Pure GOLD

To Gail —
with gratitude
for helping to
bring Pure Gold
to life!

Holli

Pure GOLD

ADVENTURES WITH
Six Rescued Golden Retrievers

HOLLI PFAU

GLAD
DOG
PRESS
DURANGO
COLORADO

Published by:
Glad Dog Press LLC
10 Town Plaza PMB #171, Durango, CO 81301

www.puregoldbook.com

Copyright © 2012 by Holli Pfau

All rights reserved. No part of this book may be reproduced or
transmitted in any form or by any means electronic or mechanical,
including photocopying, recording or by any information storage
and retrieval system without written permission from the publisher.

The *Denver Post* excerpt from "Putting on the Dog" by
Jenel Stelton-Holtmeier, appeared Monday, February 18, 2008.
Reprinted with permission.

Full article, "In Praise of Home and Heroes" by Holli Pfau originally
published in the *Durango Herald*, appeared June 27, 2001.
Reprinted with permission.

"A Day in the Life of the Dogs" is reprinted from
the *PAT Training Manual*, with the permission of
Huntington Memorial Hospital, Pasadena, California.

Editor: Gail M. Kearns, www.topressandbeyond.com
Cover Design: Diane McIntosh
Interior design by John McKercher/StudioXen
Typeset with Sabon and Sanvito

Book production coordinated by To Press & Beyond

PUBLISHER'S CATALOGING-IN-PUBLICATION DATA

Pfau, Holli.
Pure gold : adventures with six rescued golden retrievers /
Holli Pfau. — 1st ed.

p. : ill. ; cm.

ISBN: 978-0-983645I-0-8

1. Dog rescue—United States. 2. Pfau, Holli. 3. Women dog
owners—United States—Biography. 4. Golden retriever—United
States. 5. Human-animal relationships. I. Title.

HV4746 .P42 2011
636.7/0832   2011930055

Printed in the United States of America

6 5 4 3 2 1   First Edition   12 13 14 15 16 17

Contents

Contents

This book is dedicated
to the remarkable people who rescue abandoned dogs,
to the people who care for, foster and nurse them
back to health, and to the people who welcome them
into their lives and cherish each and every soul.

And most of all, to the dogs,
who reward us with love, joy and gratitude
for the gift of life.

Finding Nikki

"I can't see the street addresses," Walter said. He peered through the windshield wipers, while rain pelted down and made the February afternoon even darker.

"Slow down, I think I see her, there on the curb," I said to my husband.

Sure enough, a small, fluffy golden puppy balanced on the curb, tiptoeing though the rain, at the end of a slender blue leash. A young teenager guided her and smiled shyly at us. We parked and stepped forward into our future.

Nikki was a beautiful pup, just three months old, medium gold in color, with a dense coat and soulful brown eyes. A product of backyard breeding, she was one of only two puppies in her litter to survive. Seven others had been stillborn. The mother soon suffered mastitis, a painful condition that wouldn't allow her to nurse the two youngsters. The family that owned her didn't want to be bothered with just two puppies and probably would have let them die, but a neighbor happened to be a nurse and volunteered to take them in and bottle raise them. Her medical expertise saved

Nikki's life, since she was born with a cleft palate and easily could have choked on milk. But with diligent, tender care, she thrived, and the cleft healed.

The two pups grew, and their adoptive family contacted the Los Angeles chapter of Golden Retriever Rescue to help find good homes for them.

I'd always loved the look of goldens, and because Casey, my black Lab mix, was aging, I began to research the breed. Somehow, I connected with Golden Rescue and put in motion the process to find my next dog. But it wasn't easy, since I wanted a puppy or young dog, and these are seldom available. Further, the adoption process proved as complex and as thorough as that for a child. Undeterred, I persisted with applications, interviews and conversations. Then, one day, the call came.

"If you're still interested in a puppy, we may have one available for you," the rescue volunteer said. "Another woman is next in line, but she may not be able to do it at this time." That's how we came to drive clear across the city of Los Angeles on a stormy Sunday afternoon to Anaheim in Orange County to meet Nikki.

I'm the only child of parents who were also only children. I have no cousins, and very few relatives were part of my family. I made friends easily at school, but that didn't always translate into relationships just down the block or right next door. Animals filled the empty spaces of childhood loneliness.

My earliest memory is of Smudgie, a large, silver gray Persian cat that slept alongside me. He seemed almost as long as I was. Named for then prevalent smudge pots (now called orchard heaters) in southern California citrus groves, he was a wonderful animal, more dog than cat. He draped himself over the back of my father's chair in the evening. He purred when touched, and loved to eat cantaloupe and peas. I considered him a beloved early companion.

Dogs were always part of our household. Sammy, a jet-black cocker spaniel, predated my arrival. He must have had a learning disability, evidenced by the number of times he ate live toads and then delivered his stomach contents to the middle of the prized Oriental rug in the living room. He survived many close encounters with wild things, but one day, the vet told my mother there was little he could do for Sammy's most recent indiscretion, and she should take him home to die. My grandmother, a very practical woman, said, "Nonsense. Let's give him some aspirin in a bowl of tomato soup and see what happens." By the next morning, Sammy had recovered sufficiently to go out to track frogs again, and continued his hobby for a long, long time. Sometimes, common sense, home remedies and a little luck work wonders.

After Sammy, came my very own first puppy, a sweet German shepherd mix named Tammy. My mother and I picked her up in the afternoon and were introducing her to our household when my father arrived home after work. He knew we were considering the next dog, but he hadn't expected to find one at home so soon. When he opened the back porch door, Tammy was right there to greet him, all wiggling, writhing puppy. "Well, well, well. What have we here?" he said and sank to the floor to gather her up tenderly in his arms. My father loved dogs.

He also succumbed to the occasional impulse, like the Easter he arrived home with two yellow ducklings for me. I'm not sure he'd discussed this addition with my mother, but she took it well. My father built a screened-in pen for them, sank an old kitchen sink into the ground for a pond, and the youngsters thrived.

In fact, they grew up so fast that the next Easter we were blessed with a dozen freshly hatched ducklings of our own. Soon the lush dichondra ground cover, the driveway and every accessible space in the yard were covered with evidence of their thriving GI tracts. Something had to change.

We loaded all the offspring into cardboard boxes and delivered them to the L.A. Zoo. My parents were relieved, the zoo was happy, and I still had the original two, Dit and Dart, who lived to ripe old ages, in duck years. From then on, we retrieved eggs from the nest to help the pair practice population control.

Along the way, a number of parakeets and a few turtles came to live at our house. I began to assume some responsibility for them, cleaning cage bottoms and cutting up fruit for the birds. One day, I cleaned the turtle bowl, but must not have noticed that the stove's oven was on high. I set the clean bowl, with turtle, on the stovetop. There were no more turtles in my childhood.

Not content to have just domestic animals, I carried home wild ones. When I found a lethargic, impaired creature, I cradled it in my arms and presented it in the kitchen. My mother recognized a possum playing possum, and did her best not to shriek or faint, but calmly walked me outside to find a box for it. We later drove into the nearby foothills to return it to its proper home.

I must have believed all these beings were my brothers and sisters. We always treated the domestic ones like members of the family. We gave them the best medical care and mourned them when they died. But just as sun follows rain, the next animal arrived to ease the pain and enrich the household. A deep love of animals was the most important gift I received from my parents, who recognized how much they meant to me.

"We started a baby book for her, and you can write in it, too," the nurse's daughter told us. "I named her Nicole, but we also call her Nikki." I thumbed through the book and saw she was born on December 9, 1985. Her mother was Holly's Golden Muffin, her father Frazier. Two tiny paw prints, made in blue and purple ink, appeared on one page. Notes described her as "very outgoing—not aggressive to other animals. Very trusting."

We gathered up Nikki's belongings, and thanked the nurse and her family for their attentive care of this little ball of fluff. We had no idea how our lives were about to change. I settled into the car for the long drive home, but I knew Walter worried about crotchety old Casey's response to this tender little pup. As if to allay his concerns, Nikki reached across from my lap, put a comforting paw on his knee, and gazed into his face. I didn't realize it then, but that was our first glimpse into her heart.

Nikki Comes Home

For the first few weeks, we kept the two dogs separated, but allowed them to see each other. Casey seemed confused and wasn't exactly welcoming; little Nikki was unperturbed. But we couldn't go on like this, with doors closed and baby gates everywhere to keep them apart. Walter worried for Nikki's safety, but I was confident all would be well. I believed she could win Casey over with her sweetness and youth.

Saturday morning, we let Casey out one door and Nikki out another on the opposite side of the house. We pulled all the drapes, so they couldn't see us fret inside, and we held our breaths. We peered from behind the curtains, from first one room and then another. All was still and quiet. We waited some more. When next we saw them, they nosed around the yard, trotted next to each other, and started to move through life as roommates. We sighed in relief and chuckled over our protective parenting.

Nikki proved herself a very quick study in puppy obedience, and approached life with a combination of confidence and a touch of concern. Her furrowed brow could be construed as either thoughtful expression or true worry.

She was well behaved, except for the occasional chew on something interesting. I still own a tall stool that I used then at the breakfast bar. One morning, while I sat there, I felt something and heard an odd sound. The foot rung was just the right height for Nikki, and she happily gnawed on the wood. That stool still bears the marks of Nikki's sharp, little puppy teeth.

She also exhibited a penchant for snails, the common garden variety that showed up in our yard after a good rain. When scoldings couldn't change her mind, I resorted to hot pepper sauce atop a nice collection of the pests. One dip into that seasoning, and Nik decided there were better ways to spend her time than munching on squishy snails.

As good as she was, somehow we weren't ever sure she could take the next step in her growing up process. Or perhaps Walter and I weren't ready. We needed the youngster to reassure us she could handle the next challenge. I guess we wanted her to pass tests to move into the next grade, or on to a new activity or challenge.

While Casey and our other dogs had certainly been loved and well cared for, we seldom traveled with them. We embraced them as pets, but we hadn't yet explored the true depths of the human-animal bond. Nik would teach us about that. Nik knew her destiny was to become a dog of the world.

Since we did quite a bit of hiking and had started to backpack, we hoped to bring her with us. She was fine on short walks or hikes, and certainly loved to meet and greet people and other dogs along the way. We planned a road trip to Colorado and wanted to take her along, but we felt she should go on a short practice trip to "qualify." We headed to the southern Sierras and hiked in the Sequoia area. Our excursions weren't long or strenuous and Nikki did fine. She had earned her ticket to ride.

However, it was odd that we—novices at traveling with a dog—felt that she had to prove to us what she was made of. We would learn so many lessons along the way and Nikki would teach us many of them. At six months of age, her wisdom already showed. She always seemed to know the polite, proper and loving way to engage with people and animals and bring out the best in them.

Our Colorado itinerary moved from one bed and breakfast that allowed dogs to the next. On our first long day of driving from southern California, we stopped in Las Vegas for gas. It must have been well over a hundred degrees, with hardly a blade of grass in sight. But Nikki strutted down the Strip and relieved herself demurely where she could. What a gal.

When we arrived at our planned motel stop in Green River, Utah, that night, I was horrified. The seedy, run down, tenement place looked even worse inside, with a disgusting avocado green shag carpet. Who knew what lurked in the depths of that ancient rag? "I can't let my dog walk on this stuff, let alone lie on it," I said. Walter had to agree, so we pushed on.

In Grand Junction, we found a brand new Rodeway Inn. The rather elegant lobby was marble-floored and spotless. I walked in with Nikki by my side, and she approached the desk clerk as if she'd done this all her life. Poised, polite and delightful, she charmed everyone and they welcomed her with open arms. We began to see what a lady she was.

Next on the itinerary: the Sheraton Hotel in Steamboat Springs. Winter's ski slopes now sported lush, green meadows, and we appreciated this wonderful place to stretch our legs after the long drive. An outdoor pool also lured us, and we planned to take turns swimming, while the other sat with Nik in the garden. Walter dove into the glassy water and swam the length of the pool underwater. Horrified by the sudden disappearance of her family member, Nik began to bark and run for her life in the opposite direction, lest the monster swallow us all. When Walter surfaced, he could barely convince her of his safety, and hers as well.

While we spent several days at a ranch outside Steamboat Springs that didn't allow pets, Nikki lounged at a local veterinarian's office. I interviewed them mercilessly on the phone, and decided she'd be in good hands. Ever mannerly, Nik went with the staff, and Walter and I trotted off to ride horses and eat fabulous food at The Home Ranch in Clark.

At the end of the week, we returned to retrieve our retriever. Nik was never one to bound into the back of the Bronco. As a matter of fact, for her entire life, she'd place her front paws delicately on the bumper, and then roll her eyes at one of us to lift her in, please. And we did—always.

But on this day, perhaps to make clear how indignant she was that we'd left without her, no matter how kind or attentive the care, she charged out of the office after saying goodbye to her caregivers, being a lady and all, bounded off the three front steps and flew—FLEW!—into the back of the Bronco. We never saw her do it before or after. And we never boarded her again a day in her life.

Throughout Colorado, Nikki took in the sights like a seasoned traveler. One of my favorite photos shows Walter and Nikki gazing out from the Trail Ridge Road rest stop in Rocky Mountain National Park. Walter has one foot atop a short stone wall, while Nikki surveys the scene with her two front feet next to his. On other trips, we posed her next to scenic landmarks or entrance signs to national parks. Families with children, who do the same thing, smiled at our well-mannered, patient pup, probably wishing their kids behaved as well.

One evening after dinner, Nikki strolled the streets of Aspen with us. Fragrant mountain air ruffled her silken fur, as we meandered from shop to shop. "Prices really are outrageous," I said, as I peered at elegant displays of clothing, furs and jewelry. While we eyed the overpriced items in one window after another, Nikki picked up something of interest in her mouth. It didn't appear to be food because she wasn't chewing. "Come here, Nik, let me see what you have." I reached in her mouth and found a crumpled dollar bill. "People must be so wealthy here that they don't even care if they lose dollar bills on the street," Walter said.

At another lovely B&B, we parked outside the yard and brought our bags into the room. We tethered Lady Nik to a heavy metal patio chair, but she panicked when we moved out of her sight, and she began to tug after us. Despite the weighty anchor behind her, she made good time across the yard until we intervened, just in time to avert a collision with a brand new Cadillac. Lesson learned: Keep her with us.

We cruised on through the breathtaking Rocky Mountains, and decided to visit the venerable Broadmoor, an elegant grand hotel outside Colorado Springs. We planned to enjoy a leisurely lunch, since it was cool enough for Nikki to doze in the Bronco while we did. On the way there, we found a big, open field where she could romp, relieve herself, and be a dog. However, she took our directive a little too literally, and found an indulgence too coarse for her refined digestive system.

A short time later, we were about to pull up to the massive portico of the hotel to be greeted by the attentive valets. Just then, Nikki announced her indigestion, and brought up the offending substance across the console and between the front seats. It was obvious she had discovered horse poop. We aborted our dining plans, and Nikki recovered, while we cleaned the car. Today's lesson: Watch what your dog has for lunch.

Heading south, we wrapped up our journey in Durango, home of the world-famous Durango and Silverton Narrow Gauge Railroad. It was our first visit to this authentic western town, perched at the edge of the rugged San Juan Mountains. Captivated by the beauty and welcomed by the friendly folks who live there, we made note that we'd like to return. Thirteen years later, we'd make the move permanent.

Traveling with Nikki made this trip a special pleasure. At six months, she displayed a maturity way beyond her age. Her openness and interest in everything and everyone introduced us to new people and experiences. And it surely deepened the bond that was growing quickly between us.

At Christmas that year, I wrote a letter to the kind and loving family who had raised Nikki the first ninety days of her life:

> Dear Joanne:
> The holidays are a time of gift giving, and today, the day before her first birthday, we want to say thank you for the wonderful gift you gave us: Nikki.

She's the light of our lives, to say the least. She romps through our days like a ray of sunshine, her love of life and joyful spirit illuminating the darkness.

We've learned a lot about goldens and know that they truly are a breed apart in dogdom. Nikki herself is the epitome of the fine traits every golden possesses.

She's grown into a beautiful young lady dog, but not without more than her share of problems. Infection set in after she was spayed, and we nursed her for several weeks before she healed. She's prone to ear and skin problems. Last week, she had surgery to remove a malformed toenail and accompanying cyst.

We have a wonderful vet who adores her. He knows her history and often takes prophylactic action to help her along. When she didn't gain weight, he put her on a special diet. Now, he always comments on how long and shiny her coat is when he pats her sturdy, rounded sides.

He says she's small for the breed, but we all know that what Nikki lacks in size, she makes up for in heart.

She's seldom alone. When I write in my office here at home, she's always curled up at my feet under the desk. When we work in the yard, she's right there, to dig in the dirt or bound across the lawn with branches we've just trimmed off. Wherever we are, she is, too.

She's given Casey, our black Lab, a new lease on life. He was twelve when she arrived and had been an only dog for about six years. At first, he was horrified, stunned by her presence, and most annoyed. Walter described Casey's situation as the seventy-year-old bachelor whose home has been invaded by a teenager playing rock music all day. But Nikki won the old guy over.

Today, at thirteen, Casey has arthritis and hip problems, cloudy vision and little hearing. But she's changed his life. She's taught him how to play again and how to run, as best he can. He's more alert and has learned to rely on her for clues to sounds. He even lets her sleep on his bed when she wants to.

Whenever we can, we take Nikki with us. She loves to go to nearby Will Rogers Park and watch the polo matches. I introduced her to horses early, since we hope to own a ranch and horses in the future. She's right at home wandering around in the stables or going nose-to-nose with a friendly steed.

She hikes, camps and sails with us. I think she likes camping best, where she can establish her territory around the campsite and greet everyone who comes by.

We took her with us to Colorado this summer, and we spent three weeks and thirty-five hundred miles together in the Bronco. My parents thought we were crazy, and other people questioned how we'd manage, with hotels, restaurants and all.

She was a delight to have along and added a whole new dimension to the experience. In that part of the world, pets are much more accepted and we never had any problem finding places to stay. She slept with us in country inns and marched through the lobbies of fine hotels. She made friends everywhere she went. Watching her bound through green meadows and splash in mountain streams made my heart sing.

Nikki loves people and animals, and especially small children. She has lovely manners, except when her enthusiasm overwhelms her and she jumps for affection. She's sensitive, playful and smart.

She thrives on touch. No matter where we are, she wants to be right there, too, touching. She soaks up love like a sponge and always wants more. Some of that is genetic. Some of that is what makes Nikki herself. But I strongly believe that much of her love and trust for human and other beings comes from her early environment and the love you lavished on her when she was a helpless pup. We're so grateful for those hours all of you spent feeding and nursing her. We reap the benefits every day.

Our love and thanks to you, your daughter and your husband for our Nikki. We'll think of you tomorrow when she's one year old.

By now, we'd recognized some remarkable traits in this young dog. I wasn't yet sure where she'd lead me, but it was evident that her big heart and deep soul were going to take me somewhere I'd never been before.

Life Changes

Nikki and I approached milestones in our lives. She'd be a year old, and I was coming up fast on forty. If the stars could align for both of us, miracles lay ahead. I didn't know what they were, but Nikki was quietly confident in the future.

After eighteen years in marketing and advertising, working at breakneck speed, I yearned for something different, but I didn't know what. Searching for something of deeper value, I reached out in volunteer work and classes to explore new options. Because I believed deeply in the relationship between people and dogs, I volunteered with Canine Companions for Independence. I took extension courses at UCLA in psychology. I read about the new field of animal-assisted therapy and wondered if that held some promise. I was ready for a sea change in my professional life.

Wherever Nikki went, she gathered a crowd. Children, adults, toddlers and seniors enjoyed meeting her. They liked to stroke her strawberry blonde fur, admire the finger waves of curl along her back, and gaze into those soul-deep eyes.

She could bounce when it was appreciated, and be calm and comforting when that was more appropriate. She always seemed to know what was right and moved through life with a confidence and wisdom way beyond her years.

Even as a young pup, scarcely arrived in our lives, Nikki drew people to her. In an early outing to Will Rogers Park near our home, she snuggled up next to a man sitting on the sidelines of the polo field. He wrapped an arm around her and continued to watch the match. It seemed as natural as if she'd been his dog.

Her outreach was warm and genuine, and she didn't seem to be filling her own needs. Rather, she seemed to sense others' interests and desires and make herself available to them. She was unlike any other dog I'd known. I began to understand the term "old soul," often applied to people and animals with a supernatural sense of the world, as if they'd lived before and brought prior knowledge with them via reincarnation.

"I want to be able to take my dog to work with me," I said to Walter over dinner one night. He smiled at this rather simple statement, thinking I had rambled off into unexplored territory. "Really. She has something very special to share with the world and I want to do it with her."

I tried to envision a new path, a different way to contribute to the world, a more satisfying way to spend my days. I waited for some kind of a sign to tell me what to do. I didn't realize that the answer was right under my nose, and it was Nikki.

Suddenly, it dawned on me, as I caressed her soft ears and looked deep into her welcoming eyes. "Nikki," I said softly, "*you* will guide me." She grinned, as if to say, "Of course I will."

So began a six-month search for our future. I tested and consulted with a career counselor, who pointed me toward something in health and human services, maybe even medical school. I was surprised, since my first Bachelor's degree was in English from USC. But my counselor encouraged me to visit with various therapists and to peruse the DOT—Dictionary of Occupational Titles.

On a Saturday morning, in a high-ceilinged library at UCLA, a page in this huge tome jumped out at me: "Recreation Therapy." The job description explained how this college degree prepared therapists to aid people with physical, emotional, social or cognitive disabilities to improve their functional abilities through the use of leisure activities. Beyond the obvious arts, crafts and music, I saw the opportunity for animals to be a powerful therapeutic modality.

"I've found it!" I cheered that night at the dinner table. "I'm going to be a recreation therapist and take Nikki to work with me!" This got Walter's attention.

Over the next few months, I worked like a wild thing—observed therapists, applied to schools, quit my job, continued Nikki's obedience lessons, and researched everything I could find on animal-assisted therapy. It was a time of high energy, and I was propelled by a commitment to bring the benefits of the human-animal bond to those in need.

I grew up believing in the strength and comfort of my animals. I benefited in my own life from the love of dogs and cats. I'd watched this young golden retriever grow and mature before my eyes, and I recognized qualities in her that would change both our lives. Nikki was more than ready; I had to prepare to match her skills.

All the while, I read this encouraging message posted in my home office:

Until one is committed, there is hesitancy, the chance to draw back, always ineffectiveness. Concerning all acts of initiative (and creation), there is one elementary truth, the ignorance of which kills countless ideas and splendid plans: that the moment one definitely commits oneself, then providence moves, too.

All sorts of things occur to help one that would never otherwise have occurred. A whole stream of events issues from the decision, raising in one's favor all manner of unforeseen incidents and meetings and material assistance, which no man could have dreamt would have come his way.

I have learned a deep respect for one of Goethe's couplets:

Whatever you can do, or dream you can, begin it.
Boldness has genius, power and magic in it.
— W. H. Murray

I turned forty and enrolled at California State University at Northridge. I committed to a two-year curriculum to earn a Bachelor's degree in recreation therapy. Twice the age of many other students, I was focused and driven. I completed hours of volunteer practicum experience in nursing homes, hospitals, a youth-at-risk program, a program for developmentally delayed youngsters, an Alzheimer's care center, and an eating disorder clinic. Whenever facilities were receptive, I took Nikki with me. And I began to observe miracles great and small.

In nursing homes, the residents were eager to share stories of animals that had blessed their lives. In hospitals, Nikki helped to make the days seem shorter and the pain less severe for patients.

She could touch wellness and memory in Alzheimer's patients. And she did it so naturally, with such grace and charm, that she took my breath away. I was awed by her confidence and composure.

I began to joke that she was the best part of me. But that was my way of admitting that I felt insecure and unsure of myself. I soon learned that, when in doubt, just watch Nikki, and she'd guide me in just the right interaction with patients and staff. She amazed me.

One day, at a Jewish Home for the Aging, Nikki and I visited with a circle of residents in wheelchairs in the activity room on the second floor. I became involved in a conversation with a woman, while Nik continued to meet and greet others. When I surfaced from my engrossing interaction, Nik was nowhere to be seen.

I ambled out to the nurses' desk and asked if they'd seen my girl. "Oh, yes," one of the ladies replied. "I saw her get on the elevator. I thought she was with you."

Now I worried, since the elevator goes to the first floor and faces a busy street, and it also goes to the third floor. I raced downstairs, but no one had seen her. I dashed to the third floor and arrived at the nurses' desk. "Oh, there you are, Holli. We wondered where you were," said one of the dog-loving nurses. "Nikki has been up here for some time."

Apparently, she waltzed into the elevator with several people going to the third floor, got off, and joined the activity group upstairs. The therapists assumed I was nearby and allowed Nikki to work her magic alone, moving from wheelchair to wheelchair, to let residents stroke her and talk to her.

When I told this story to Walter, he laughed. "Once she learns how to take the bus, she won't need you at all."

After a year and a half of commuting to classes, scurrying home to study, taking tests, and writing papers, it was time for my internship. After some research, it was obvious that there was only one place to go: King's View Center in Reedley, near the city of Fresno in central California. Set amid rich agricultural growing areas, this in-patient psychiatric facility for acutely ill children and adults featured animals in their treatment programs. A very talented recreation therapist there, Patty Harper, oversaw an animal-assisted therapy program that included a dog, sheep, goats, horses and other assorted barnyard animals. Every morning that semester, I witnessed Mother Nature unfurl spring blossoms and nurture bountiful harvests. Calves and lambs were being born; chicks and ducklings were hatched. The promise of the season wasn't lost on me. I hoped my own professional growth would be as abundant.

Each Sunday evening, I bid my dear husband and sweet Nikki farewell and drove three hours north, often with tears spilling down my cheeks, as I felt the miles separate us. I spent each week trying to push the envelope, expand my horizons, cope with doubts, and—with luck—succeed. But the sweetest times of all were Friday nights when I pulled into my own driveway, to be welcomed home again. "It's Sweetie," Walter would announce, as he hugged me, and Nikki twirled and danced around us both.

But there was even more of a balancing act going on here. During my fieldwork hours the prior year, I'd found my way to Huntington Memorial Hospital in Pasadena, California. My professor told me he thought they had a dog that visited in the rehabilitation department. I was off in a flash to see what they were doing.

Recreation therapist and department head Maureen

Beith had set aside a bit of time from her lunch hour to meet with me. She introduced me to her dog, Chelsea, who indeed came to work with her. My eyes lit up. Here was Nikki's and my future.

During that year as a volunteer at Huntington, I met and formed an alliance with three other women, who also wanted to learn about and implement animal-assisted therapy. Jenny Hamilton sat behind me in our Introduction to Gerontology class. I was telling another student about Nikki's rounds, when Jenny leaned forward and, in her delightful New Zealand accent, said, "Oh, that sounds wonderful. I want to do that, too, and I also have a golden retriever." Jenny was studying for her Master's degree in gerontology.

Lora Williams was a fellow student in my UCLA class on abnormal psychology. After the first few weeks, we noticed that we both asked the professor and some of the patients she brought to class about the importance of animals in their lives. Without exception, these patients seemed to soften, smile and move into a more comfortable place when they spoke about animals. Lora headed one of the research departments at Mattel Toys.

Maggie Crawford volunteered in the rehabilitation unit at Huntington and observed the benefits of patient interactions with Chelsea. Maggie would go on to earn her Master's degree in counseling, often accompanied by her golden retrievers.

We formed a committee, researched other programs across the country, became experts on the array of issues pertinent to bringing dogs into a large acute care hospital, and started a pilot program. We were blessed with a welcoming administration at the hospital, a supportive advisory committee of doctors and staff members, and three wonderful dogs that formed the backbone of a program that began in 1987 and continues to this day. At its largest, PAT (pet-assisted therapy) at Huntington served all units in the hospital (except emergency) with forty teams of carefully screened, well-trained volunteers and their own dogs.

While I interned in Reedley, I remained part of the pilot program at Huntington, and tried to keep all parts of my life alive and well.

I felt overwhelmed, lost and incompetent at Kings View. Surrounded by more than twenty superb clinicians, including horticulture therapists, music therapists, an art therapist and, of course, recreation therapists, I felt way out of my league. They all seemed so competent, so sure of themselves. I had years of life experience, but in a vastly different profession. Here my age seemed to be a double-edged sword. People assumed I knew more and had greater confidence in my skills. Nothing was further from the truth.

I questioned my abilities every day. Was I able to evaluate patients, assess their needs, and develop a treatment plan with creative and appropriate therapeutic interventions? It all seemed well beyond my reach. I found it hard to leap the chasm between classroom learning and clinical application.

And I'd never really spent much time around young people. Now, I was assigned to the children's unit, to work with severely traumatized and disturbed kids. I felt like an imposter.

I agonized over everything and yearned to be back home, where I could be encouraged by Walter and work with Nikki, who by now I was positive wasn't only the best part of me, but the only good thing I had going for me.

Several weeks before I departed for my internship, a film crew from CBS Evening News came to Huntington to film our fledgling program. The producer had two golden retrievers of his own and understood how this visitation program would benefit everyone at the hospital. He spent a day with Maggie, Jenny and me and our three goldens, while we visited patients in oncology, rehab and a medical/surgical unit. We knew the finished piece would air sometime in the next month.

Back at King's View, it was my birthday, and I felt especially sorry for myself. I sat in the activity room well past the end of the workday, ate a microwaved frozen dinner, and wallowed in a self-imposed sea of incompetence. Despite a near 4.0 grade average, strong recommendations from my professors, and months of productive fieldwork hours, I thought I was on the verge of failure.

Suddenly, I heard Dan Rather talk about the dogs at Huntington. I looked up at the television that hummed in the background to see my friends, our dogs, and yes, myself in the familiar halls of the hospital. We visited with patients and heard staff members praise our efforts.

It was as if dark skies had parted and God himself sent light into the room. In those few moments, I received the best birthday gift imaginable: validation of my passion and resurrection of my commitment to bring something special to those in need. A network TV anchor and my friends and colleagues rescued me. It was time to move forward, cast aside these silly doubts, and get on with the business of the future. I had to live up to Nikki's talents and give mine a chance.

Nikki's Career

I stood at the top of the driveway that leads into the rehabilitation unit, and took a deep breath. "Now, you have to be a good girl, pay attention, and do all the right things," I said to Nikki, who danced beside me. "I don't know exactly what we'll do, but I know you'll make people happy." Her tongue lolled out one side, she smiled her widest grin, and all but said, "So, let's get on with it!"

This was our first day as a volunteer team at Huntington, and I could hardly contain my excitement. We'd just spent a year in meetings, had written and secured approvals for protocols, and explained the concept of animal-assisted therapy to the staff. Most were eager to see the dogs and enthusiastic about this new, unique service for their patients.

Chelsea had been the true pioneer dog on the rehab unit, so we weren't a novelty there. However, patients in oncology, orthopedics and a medical/surgical unit had only heard about the canine "therapists." These three units plus rehab had been selected as sites for our pilot program and research study.

When Nik trotted down the hall, she elicited smiles,

waves, many pats on the head, hugs and even embraces from staff members, who sat down on the floor and wrapped their arms around her. She took the exuberance in stride and smiled right back at everyone.

"Oh, you must come see Mrs. Johnson right away," said a therapist. "She's been waiting for you."

"No, I think you should stop to see my patient in 12A," countered the speech therapist. "I just know she'll find it easier to talk to the dog than to me."

"Wait—what about my patient who wants to brush Nikki?" asked the occupational therapist. "I told her you'd be here soon."

It was obvious we'd need to budget our time, work with everyone to establish priorities, and try hard to meet expectations. Nik stood in the center of the hallway by the busy nurses' station and welcomed all comers. "Bring it on!" her eyes said.

That day was typical of the time we spent on the units. We moved from room to room, all the while stopping to visit with families, visitors, nurses, doctors and administrators. We soon learned that although hallway visits were neither planned nor logged in patients' charts, they were just as important to dog lovers and patients in need of attention. If we could break the "chain of stress" that so many staffers seemed to carry with them throughout the day, we knew their next encounter with a patient would be quieter, calmer and more effective.

Sometimes, white-coated figures dashed down a hallway, preoccupied and purposeful. But even they would pause for a brief encounter with us, or just trail a gentle hand down Nikki's back when they passed by. We knew those moments were meaningful, too.

All three dogs in the pilot program—Monty, Saffron and Nikki—were golden retrievers. This wasn't planned, but certainly was serendipitous. Their big hearts, deep brown eyes and soft, flowing coats seemed destined for this work. After they learned the routine in rehab, the teams would move on to their designated units for the pilot program.

In rehab, we had some flexibility in our schedule, and opportunities abounded for interactions all over the unit. Patients who walked to regain their strength and balance liked to have Nikki lead them down one of the outdoor pathways or across an uneven surface like the grass. If a small group was planting flowers in raised beds from their wheelchairs, most of them welcomed a visit. Physical and occupational therapists would schedule us as part of a half-hour treatment session, when a patient could brush Nik, fasten and unfasten her collar and leash, or walk toward her in the parallel bars. Nik was a destination and a reward for many patients who loved dogs, and she sometimes provided better motivation than even the finest therapist could conjure.

We had no restrictions on the unit, except that the dogs couldn't be present whenever food was served. We could work in the activity room until meal trays arrived, and then we'd have to leave until they were removed. One day, while I visited with staff at the nurses' station and received the day's assignments, Nikki seemed content to stand by my side and watch the passing parade. Engrossed in discussion about a patient, I didn't notice that my leash had become a little more taut, and that Nik was perusing the returned trays on the meal cart outside the dining room. She must have been astonished to see the bounty at her eye level that would go to waste. Delicately, being a lady, of course, she slipped her nose into a tray of uneaten roast beef and potatoes and dined.

Suddenly, I realized what was happening and, horrified, pulled her away, relieved that she'd cleaned up leftovers and hadn't scarfed down someone's fresh meal. Lesson learned: Never take my eyes off her when meal trays could entice her again.

But other temptations awaited. A physician in rehab persisted in bringing "treats" to the dogs, usually pieces of bacon or toast from the cafeteria. No matter how many times we reminded her that the dogs weren't allowed to snack on the job, she continued to ignore our protocols. Sometimes, patients would squirrel away tasty morsels in their bedside dresser drawers and bring them out when we visited. Once Nikki was offered a cold pork chop wrapped in a napkin, and I'm sure she would have indulged had I not restated the rules. "No, thank you very much, though. She has to keep her figure trim."

We met people from all walks of life. One morning, a gentleman sat on the edge of his bed, waiting for his discharge from the hospital. His eyes lit up when we walked in, and I soon learned that he'd been a judge at dog shows. "Would you like me to judge her for you?" he asked. "Why, of course. We'd be delighted," I replied. We set Nik atop his bed and he stacked her neatly, all four paws aligned in a perfect rectangle. "A lovely top line," he murmured, "and what nice flaps." I looked puzzled and admitted that I didn't know what flaps were. "It's her lip line and her jowls," he said, absorbed in running his hands over her beautiful coat and firm body. "She's a lovely dog," he said with a smile. "Yes, I'm grateful to have her in my life."

Another day, we walked into the activity room and were met by a woman who inched toward us in a wheelchair, her head wrapped in bandages with a small scarf over them.

With great effort, she reached toward Nikki and looked up at me. In a deep voice, she said, "I want to kiss her on the nose." "I'm sure she'd love that," I said. The woman leaned forward ever so slowly and grasped Nik's head between her trembling hands. Steady as a rock, Nik received this intimate expression from a total stranger. "Thank you," the woman said in her gravely voice, and then rolled on down the hallway. We never saw her again.

From that first day in the hospital, I learned to trust my dog—except around food. Her sensitivity to peoples' needs and emotions was unerring. She responded to young children with energetic wiggles and tail wags. Enthusiastic visitors could usually engage her in spirited interactions. But she could also sit still in a chair at a comatose patient's bedside and watch me lift the patient's hand and stroke her with it.

One afternoon, we traveled down a hallway between units and saw a bereaved family leave a patient's room. The nurse beside them motioned to me to pause, and we watched to see what would happen next. The older woman, with tears streaming down her face, sank to the floor and wrapped her arms around Nikki. Together they sat for several moments and let stillness envelope them both. Nikki leaned into her, to absorb the emotion, and didn't budge. Then, the woman stroked the golden head, whispered a few words that only Nik could hear, and stood and rejoined her family. Her slight smile to me spoke volumes.

Some patients sang to Nikki; some wrote poetry and read it to her. Children drew pictures and shared them. People laughed, cried and told her their innermost thoughts. Some never spoke at all, but preferred to have her stretch out full length alongside them on the bed and breathe in unison. Some patients were recovering; some were dying.

They were all the same to Nikki, and she approached them with gracious unanimity.

Maggie, Jenny and I taught our dogs the skills they'd need to reach, engage and support patients. They had to heel close to us, stay out of the way of people and equipment, ignore the oddest of sights and smells, and sit, down and stay on command. We also taught them "paws up," to put their front feet lightly on a patient's bedside and wait to be lifted into position. This could be a delicate maneuver if we had to accommodate IV lines, catheters, pillows that protected incision sites, and all manner of bandages and monitors.

While we taught techniques, the dogs taught us deeper lessons. We didn't want to tire patients beyond their limits, and we'd often say something like, "I think we should leave, so you can get some rest." Sometimes, the patient agreed, but other times our dogs would lean into the patient and cast eyes upward toward us that said, "No, not yet." We often saw this in oncology, when a patient had a difficult day and needed extra comfort from an understanding canine. We learned to listen to our dogs.

They also led us into unplanned encounters. One afternoon, a woman drew two of us with our dogs into a patient's room. It soon became apparent that the woman was more in need of a visit than her sister who was the patient. Jenny sat next to her and listened to her wrestle with her sister's impending death. Nik and I settled at the patient's bedside and heard about the peace and acceptance that had come into her life now, as it was about to end. A single team couldn't have managed such disparate emotions, but the two of us were able to listen, comfort and validate all feelings in the room.

There were also surprises. When a dog barked in the hallway (a no-no for sure), call lights and buzzers began to go off at the nurses' station. Patients who were unfamiliar with our program said, "I thought I heard a dog bark! What's going on?" Of course, that just elicited a number of new requests for visits.

Not everyone wanted to see the dogs, and we respected their feelings, although we didn't understand them one bit. Occasionally, overzealous nurses would grab us when we arrived on the unit and steer us into a patient's room, unannounced. "Get that damn dog out of here!" was one unexpected response. "Oh, that's a very good thing," the nurse told us, as we beat a hasty retreat. "That's the most we've heard out of him since he got here. Now, we have something to talk about."

Holidays were special, because we tried to bring the spirit of the season into the clinical setting. Everyone chuckled at Halloween when we put a few costume items on the dogs and paraded through the halls. Christmas meant antler headgear and red and green taffeta neckties and bows. We made rounds as Santa Paws and the Reindogs, often with homemade shortbread cookies shaped like dog bones for the staff. Nikki became Saint Nik for the day.

The more I worked alongside Nikki, the deeper my respect for her grew. Several people described her as an "old soul." At first, I didn't know what that meant. But I discussed it, read some, and came to appreciate the concept of reincarnation. An old soul is one who has experienced several lifetimes already and brings the wisdom and knowledge from those experiences into the present day. Perhaps that did explain the depth of her soul and tenderness of her interactions. Very little disturbed her. She approached every new encounter with grace, and always gave me confidence when I felt uncertain and unsteady.

Once our training period ended in rehab, Nikki and I were assigned to the oncology unit for the pilot program. I had no prior experience with cancer patients, either in my personal life or my studies. But in her true fashion, Nikki showed me the way.

We spent much of our time with families, while they waited outside their loved ones' rooms, contemplated what was to come, and how they would cope. Nikki's openness and genuine interest in each person made her a safe recipient for these fears and worries. Somehow, people could look into her deep brown eyes, share their darkest thoughts, and feel comforted.

With patients, she could be playful or pensive, as needed. One of her favorites was Julie, a young woman hospitalized often for surgery, chemotherapy, radiation or the combined side effects of the aggressive treatment. "Oh, here's Nikki!" she'd exclaim, and slide over in bed to smooth the linens, so Nikki would have room to stretch out next to her. Julie was usually forthcoming about her treatment and how she felt, but always kept much of the focus on Nikki during our visits. She also taught us something special.

"You know what I do at night sometimes, when I'm scared or can't sleep?" she asked me one day. "I spread out my blanket and stroke it as if it were Nikki, and that helps me to feel better." Nik was able to help even when she wasn't there.

Patients in the infusion room, who sat through long hours of chemotherapy, always welcomed the diversion of my golden girl. We heard many stories of beloved pets, family gatherings, future plans and the pleasures of good company. Nik was, of course, the catalyst of all this and seemed to revel in her role as social butterfly and group facilitator.

We were on our way.

Dogs On Call

The program grew, we recruited and trained more volunteers, and added new units to our visiting schedule. I joined the staff as a recreation therapist and supervised the program under the aegis of the volunteer department. Volunteer director Priscilla Gamb and her staff were gracious and supportive and didn't mind sharing their offices with our furry partners.

Nurses clamored for more time for their patients with the dogs. We enjoyed this enviable position, and were grateful for the success of the pilot program and growth into new areas. But Maggie, Jenny and I will always remember those early, long, exciting and exhausting days when it was just the three of us with our three goldens, when we began to make a difference.

I wrote of those days in our volunteer training manual. The names of patients and staff have been changed. Only the names of our dogs and the PAT volunteers are real. We preserved anonymity and patient confidentiality, so we could share the essence of our days in the hospital with our partners.

A Day in the Life of the Dogs

We walk into Karen's room and notice the heavy smell of infected tissue hanging in the air. We anticipate her gentle smile, but instead, wide, frightened eyes and sunken cheeks greet us.

The dogs are eager to engage with the young woman they'd come to know over months of weekly visits, but she's too agitated and distracted to focus on them. The two dogs curl up in the corner of the room and wait, and Jenny and I lean over Karen's bed to hear her weak voice.

But we can't understand her. Anxiety, medications and disease have robbed her of coherence, and we struggle to make sense of the sounds. All the while, we try to calm and comfort her. We bring a fresh gown and top sheet. We brush her hair and put Vaseline on her lips. Jenny sees a bottle of perfume on the dresser and dabs fragrance on Karen's throat and wrists. I rub her thin shoulder.

We leave with the two golden retrievers, who wag and smile up at her, and I remind Karen to think of the dogs and look at their pictures on her wall when she feels lonely.

Jenny and I walk across the hall to join Maggie, who is visiting Mrs. Smyth. Now ninety, she first met the dogs last summer, and loves to talk with us, while the dogs curl around her chair. Last week, she told Maggie that her time had come and she wanted to die.

But this morning she looks better, swathed in white blankets in a chair beside her bed. Our two dogs, Nikki and Honey, trot in to join Monty, and Mrs. Smyth welcomes them all. Despite her failing vision and hearing, she and Maggie conversed for half an hour. She recounted clearly the story of a small spaniel she once owned, who became the surrogate mother for a litter of kittens.

Tired now, she thanks us for coming, and asks us to keep her in our thoughts. She wants to go to sleep, finally. We promise to do this and leave her sitting in the chair, still hoping to end her long life peacefully.

In the hall, we talk briefly of the visits and recompose ourselves, to continue cheerfully on to our next patients.

Jenny begins a visit with Mr. Damon, an elderly gentleman with Parkinson's disease. She places Honey's front paws on the edge of the bed, so the patient can see and touch her soft fur with little effort. They're talking quietly when Maggie and I stop at the doorway, greeted by the roaring laughter of the other patient in the room. The jolly gentleman is so bemused by the presence of dogs in the hospital that he guffaws, great thigh-slapping guffaws, when he sees us. He'd announced to his nurse that he didn't want to request a dog visit, but could he order up some pretty young women instead? He roars with laughter. We smile and continue down the hall, to lessen the noise and distraction for Jenny's quiet, earnest visit.

That was a Monday morning in January 1990, on a general medical and surgical unit at Huntington Memorial Hospital, fourteen months after we began the PAT program of pet-assisted therapy. Our four golden retrievers have spent countless hours snuggled on beds, sitting on chairs, and wagging in hallways. They've interacted with young and old, sick and well, patients and staff. They cheer the lonely, comfort the frightened, and bring smiles to just about everyone.

No two days are the same. We arrive with the dogs to help. We go where we're needed, and do what we can. It's always a challenge, sometimes painful, and without exception rewarding. This day was a potpourri, as usual.

Barbara, head nurse, dog lover and friend, stands at the nurses' station, as we funnel out of the stairwell and onto the unit. The dogs all know and love her, and crowd around for affection. Barbara plans to adopt a retiring guide dog soon. The dog, Katie, has been staying at the hospital with her blind owner through the woman's recent surgeries. Barbara and twelve-year-old Katie found each other and soon she'll begin her new career as a member of the PAT program. Busy staff member Barbara always finds time to sit on the floor in the hall, play with our dogs, and explain the therapeutic benefits of the human-animal bond to all who pass by.

An elderly couple waits by the elevator outside the volunteer office. The woman holds a small, elegant arrangement of yellow roses and white ribbons. The three of us, with dogs, head out the adjacent door and down the hall. They watch us and smile when we explain our mission.

Just then, the dogs spot a youngster in the hall with Diana, one of the hospital's child life specialists. Along with love and tennis balls, the dogs all fancy children, so we're literally drawn toward nineteen-month-old Jessica, who takes in the scene with wide brown eyes. She settles on the floor and we put all the dogs on "down stay." Diana guides the child's actions, asks questions, and encourages interactions. We invite her to make an appointment with us to see Jessica each week and she agrees to call us.

I look up to see the elderly couple again, without flowers now, as they walk slowly by, watching the youngster with the dogs. Again, they smile at the dogs and pass a talkative and friendly crowd of interns, who turn the corner and join our group. We've met them all, and I ask one young man how he's doing with his puppy. He rolls his eyes and says, "He chewed up my ID badge and my stethoscope!"

When we left Jenny with Mr. Damon earlier in the day, Maggie and I moved on to the oncology unit to check our visitation schedule. Busy staff members swirl in and out of the nurses' station and greet the dogs' arrival. Before we can check patient names and room numbers, we meet Mrs. Harmon, who stands just outside the flurry of activity.

A composed but anxious woman in her seventies, she awaits word from her husband's biopsy that morning. Our instincts are right in pausing to chat and ask gentle questions. She's eager to talk and we learn her husband's medical history, including the heart attack, aneurysm, brain surgery and tumors of the past decade. They'll celebrate their forty-ninth anniversary in April and are best friends. She looks worried.

She strokes the dogs' heads and talks and appears to relax. We offer understanding and she shares her faith in God. We promise to check back with her later in the afternoon.

When meals arrive for patients, we leave the unit. It's a good time for our own lunch. First, we take the dogs outside to the grass and ivy for their break, and then settle them in the conference room in the volunteer office. We pick up our lunches in the cafeteria, along with extra cups of water for the dogs, and return to eat with them. Sometimes, we discuss the morning's visits. Sometimes, we share about our own lives. Sometimes, we just talk about the dogs.

This particular Monday is a bit of everything. The goldens crowd around their bowl, filled with fresh water. They slurp and drip water on each other's heads and necks. Refreshed, they each pick a cool spot on the linoleum floor and settle down for a nap. With their thick, luxuriant coats, they're often warm in the units and on patients' beds. Lunch hour is a welcome break.

Oncology continues to be a busy place at 2:00 PM. Nurses from the morning shift prepare to hand off status reports to the on-coming shift of nurses. Results from morning tests are in and staff members consult with doctors on changes in treatment. Family members hover to learn details about their patients. A physical therapist reads a chart before meeting with the patient. And we arrive with the dogs.

At the nurses' station, Maggie notices a cart filled with flower arrangements and recognizes Mr. Barrett's name on the cards. We'd visited this lovely man several times before, and Maggie asks if he's moved to another room, since we look forward to seeing him today. One of the nurses tells her that he died at noon.

Maggie shares the news with us and we exchange looks of shock and dismay. She speaks what we all thought: "We should have seen him this morning." We know better than that. Still, it was what we felt right then.

There's little time to indulge our own feelings during a visitation day. So, we each stash our thoughts away, to be reconciled later, and begin more visits.

First stop is Peter, who is seventeen. He has leukemia and is in isolation. But we pause in the doorway, so he can see the dogs, and take a Polaroid picture of them for his bulletin board.

Kara is just across the hall. She has teenage boys and a house and yard full of animals. We've visited her several times and she's been troubled by her speech difficulties. But today, things are better. Her friend shepherds us all inside and we quickly put two dogs on chairs alongside the bed. Kara reaches toward them both. She initiates conversation and inquires about the dogs. She smiles.

Just then, her doctor arrives. "Well, how nice to see all of you, dogs included," he says. "I've heard so much about these dogs, but this is the first time I've seen them in person. Tell me more about your program."

We summarize our protocols for him. "Our veterinarian conducts behavioral testing and health screenings. The dogs are bathed and groomed within twenty-four hours of visiting. We submit stool samples to the hospital for testing. We check with the nurses to be sure it's okay to visit a patient. We always put a clean sheet on top of the patient's bed, to catch any shed hair. And last thing before we leave, we bring a soapy washcloth for the patient to wipe her hands."

"Be sure to come back soon," Kara's doctor says. "I think these beautiful dogs can really make a difference in the hospital. It looks like you've made Kara's day. Why, I feel better myself."

We prepare to leave the two of them alone. Before we go, we tell Kara how good she looks and promise a longer visit next week. Again she smiles. So do we.

I look in Mr. Harmon's room. He's alone with a chaplain.

I back away from the doorway, and note the room number for next week's visits.

Jenny and Maggie have gone on to see Bonnie, an old friend. A year ago, at the start of our program, Bonnie was photographed with Monty for the local newspaper. Since then, she's managed to avoid sickle cell crisis, until this week. Hospitalized for hydration and pain control, she has an intravenous line in her right arm, but is bright-eyed and jubilant to see the dogs again. She regales everyone with stories about the newspaper article and photo, and shares her plans to do peer counseling and education for sickle cell patients. Nikki and I join the gathering and Bonnie becomes buried under a blanket of dogs on her bed. Her hands never leave the dogs, and she talks to each like a friend. It's hard to leave this island of joy in a unit often marked by sadness and pain.

Our last visit here is planned with Susie. This twenty-seven-year-old beauty has cancer, everywhere. Over the months, we've watched her suffer and strive, and rally and lose ground. We ask to see Susie, but she declines due to weakness.

She has a wonderful support system of family and friends, mostly women. Today, we find her mother and grandmother in the unit lounge, drained and dazed. We stand at the lounge doorway, uncertain whether to enter, until one of our dogs marches straight in, followed by the other dogs and, of course, us. Each dog selects a person to attach to and we follow suit.

It's a heart-rending half hour. Susie's mother finds enough energy to express anger and rage at this wicked disease. Susie asks to see her and she leaves the room.

Susie's gentle, Southern grandmother shares stories about her granddaughter—as a child, as a teenager, as a lovely young woman. They're much alike, she says. With pride, she tells us how she was able to send Susie to Paris last year for three weeks. She smiles at the memories, but tears spill down her cheeks. Nikki snuggles closer and the frail woman strokes the golden head.

One of Susie's young friends, very tall, brunette and pretty, joins us. Susie has asked for her grandmother. The eighty-year-old woman's face crumples. She asks us how she can possibly do this. Jenny reminds her of her strength and love for Susie. Maggie reminds her that the pain is bearable with the love. I help her to her feet.

Slowly, she walks to the doorway, one arm around Susie's friend, the other steadied on a wooden cane. She's so tiny, the brunette so tall. Together they go to say goodbye to Susie. We sit with the dogs in painful silence. We try not to cry. Jenny reminds us to breathe deeply. We leave the family, the friends and Susie.

We each go separately to see the last patients on our schedule. Maggie and I return to the morning's unit to see two women. In this late afternoon, both are quiet and receptive to our visits. Elderly and quite sick, both display a degree of acceptance—small, still women lying peacefully under crisp white sheets. They trust us to bring the dogs alongside the beds. Helen enjoys having Monty curl up on the bed, right behind the curve of her knees. Mildred seems amused by Nikki's very presence. She has porcelain skin and delft blue eyes, and likes me to warm her cold hands in mine.

Jenny visits a middle-aged man in orthopedics, who is recovering from an auto accident. He enjoys Honey and they look forward to seeing each other next week.

Back in the volunteer office, we doggedly write progress notes on each visit of the day. We log patients by unit and file consent forms and our notes. We're obviously getting punchy, losing pages, notes and our thoughts. We laugh at our bumblings. The concrete nature of the task and the humor help to relieve the tension of the day. The dogs have been outside to the ivy, had quenching drinks, and roam comfortably in the office.

At 6:30 PM, we finally don our coats, turn out the lights, and lock the office door behind us. After signing out, we turn down the long hall to the exit. The dogs trot knowingly toward the parking lot, home and dinner. Just near the entrance, we meet a young father with his blonde daughter and son. All three are fascinated with the dogs and, once again, we're on the floor together. The toddler finally gains the courage to pat Monty's ear, while his sister ceremoniously hugs all three dogs. Maggie asks if this helps to make the hospital a better place and the father agrees, saying to his children, "Weren't we lucky to see the dogs?"

The last person we meet is another young man, who is drawn to the dogs. He kneels to scratch Nikki's ear and asks the basic question: "What are the dogs here for?"

"To visit patients and help them feel better," I reply, condensing the past eight hours and fourteen months into one sentence.

Epilogue

We try to follow our patients for the duration of their hospitalization, even when they're moved to other units. We feel a bond and like to know how they're doing. We also want to know when one of our new friends has died. It helps us to close a chapter in our book here at the hospital.

- Karen died later in the week before our next visit. We heard from a night nurse how much she loved the dogs and how much the visits meant to her.
- Mrs. Smyth improved and was discharged to a nursing home.
- Peter was discharged to his home and treatment will continue. We expect to see him again.
- Kara died, after many weeks in the hospital.
- Susie asked to be discharged the same evening that we visited. She died peacefully at home five days later, with her family and her dog.

We haven't heard about our other friends. We hope they're well.

Bodie

"He seems a little goofy to me. What do you think?" I ask Walter. We watch the collection of young dogs, a few adults and one gangly, distracted pup romp in the breeder's backyard.

"I think he's a fine dog. I think we should take him."

"I'm just not sure yet. Let's think about it." We thank Joan and promise to call.

After Casey, our elderly black Lab mix, died, Nikki lived for a brief time as an only dog. She probably would have been fine with that, as mature and worldly as she was, but we weren't. We'd come to enjoy the interactions and energy of two dogs, and began to look for the next golden to join our family.

As luck would have it, Joan, a breeder of goldens, lived just over the hill and up a canyon from us in Pacific Palisades. This small bedroom community perches on cliffs above the Pacific, located between Santa Monica and Malibu. Canyons funnel traffic east and west, from the beach up to manicured gardens and sunny properties.

Through some local networking, I learned that one of Joan's puppies had been brought back to her. Uh oh.

Something must be wrong. And indeed it was, but with the first owner, not the dog.

Bo had been purchased with his sister, but was soon returned. "There's something wrong with his eye—he's not perfect," had been the reason, or excuse, for not keeping this lanky blond boy.

On further examination, Bo was diagnosed with entropion, an abnormal condition where the edge of the eyelid turns inward, and the lashes irritate and can eventually damage the cornea. A veterinary ophthalmologist could perform surgery and he'd be good as new. We hoped.

But I still wasn't sure about Bo. He did seem goofy, all legs and lack of focus. He flopped around the yard, disoriented at being returned and having to regain his place in the pack. I wasn't sure he had the right stuff to be a therapy dog. I wanted to sleep on it.

We departed as planned for a long vacation in the Yellowstone region, to enjoy the wilderness and wildlife in one of America's most dramatic and remote national parks. Walter describes the area within a hundred-mile radius of the park as some of the best in the world for fly-fishing, wildlife photography, and wilderness hiking and backpacking. We've seen it buried in the depths of winter snow, flushed with autumn colors, and abundant with summer wildflowers. We never tire of discovering a moose with calf in the willows or hearing a bull elk bugle at dusk for his harem. Immersed in the wild, I didn't really think about Bo.

We came home and, for some odd reason, I hadn't yet been in touch with the breeder. A month passed and perhaps I expected or feared that he'd found another home.

The phone rang. "Hi Holli, it's Joan. I just want to let you know that Bo is still here, and he's waiting for you."

Sometimes, decisions are made for you, and apparently, this was one of them. If he was still without a home, perhaps we were meant to be together. I drove over the hill to take another look at the young man.

A little less goofy now, and re-acclimated to Joan's kennel environment, Bo sauntered out to greet me. Yes, he was more interactive, I noticed, and less distracted by everything around him. Maybe he could be a therapy dog after all. He loped into the Bronco and into our hearts as well.

A silvery ash blond, he was quite a stunning dog. Yes, at six months, he still had a lot of growing to do, but was handsome already. Long-bodied, lithe and lean, he had a tail like a plume, and carried it proudly. It could clear a coffee table of everything except the heaviest books, so some adjustments in home décor were in order. Deep, dark pools of brown eyes were set off by his silver fur, which made his eyes seem even more magical. Atop his skull, a quite pronounced occipital bone protruded. We began to refer to that as the extra space he needed for his brain, although his ranginess and wide grin belied his modest capabilities.

Nik welcomed him without hesitation, as if they were destined to be together. She tried to introduce him to the household, to apply her standards of decorum, but to no avail. His length and still developing coordination often left him looking a little silly, next to her polite and precise style. We began to call them The Countess and The Cowboy—she all frills and femininity, and he way more John Wayne than Cary Grant. They were the perfect couple.

I wanted to get Bo up to speed as quickly as possible in obedience and preparations to be a good hospital dog, so we enrolled in puppy class, and I started to take him on walks in the community. On our first foray through the little village, we walked past the car wash one morning when suddenly, all the equipment fired up at once, pumps and engines blasting into action. Not exposed to much outside Joan's yard, poor Bo was apoplectic. He collapsed on the ground as if he'd been shot. It was all I could do to get him on his feet and walking again. *Oh, dear. Maybe this is a terrible mistake.* He didn't appear able to regain his composure. What will he do when he sees a giant x-ray machine wheeled down the hallway, or when a fire alarm goes off?

But unlike his first family, I wasn't going to give up on the lad. He deserved a better shot at a good life and we were going to give it to him. With some trepidation, we scheduled the eye surgery. He came through it like a champ, barely noticing the stitches in his eyelid. Once healed, his former "defect" was never a problem again. He was now perfect and on his way.

His given name was Bo, or perhaps Beau, neither of which seemed sufficient for him. And when I needed to discipline him, calling out "Bo, no" or "No, Bo" just didn't work for me. On our next trip to the Sierras, however, we christened him with his new name: Bodie. How very appropriate, that this silver-frosted golden with boundless energy and high spirits be named after a once wild and crazy mining town just east of the High Sierra mountains. At the end of thirteen miles of wash-boarded dirt road, Bodie State Historic Park now protects the remains of the original town once known as one of the rowdiest in the West. Historians report that a young girl, preparing to move with her family to the outpost camp said, "Goodbye God, I'm going to Bodie." Our rambunctious young golden would have fit right in.

We continued to enjoy our wilderness outings. We started Bodie off right away hiking and exploring the high country near Mammoth Lakes. It was obvious he was born to race up hills, charge down steep trails, and sniff out water a mile away—and then dive into it with an enthusiasm and energy that always made us smile. If we hiked five miles, he did double or triple that, always in a hurry to see what was around the next bend, and he raced back to lead us onward. He had the heart of an athlete and the spirit of the wild.

Always more content to trot close to our footsteps, Nikki would probably have preferred to lounge at the campsite, if truth were told. We envisioned her more like Scarlett in *Gone with the Wind,* faintly fanning herself and proclaiming " My, my, but it's warm today," then swooning backward onto an elegant velvet settee.

We tried to accommodate their differences in our outings. Hikes of modest length to a lake gave Bodie the chance to get his mileage in, and added hours of water play to his workout. Nik could saunter along with us, pause to take in the scenery or a fragrant patch of wildflowers, and still make it to the lunch stop on time. By then, Bodie had put in a full day's effort, but considered it just a warm-up for an intense game of fetch in a frigid lake, fed by recent snowmelt.

No matter the size of stick, branch or small log that we hurled into the water, Bodie would swim like a maniac to get it and haul it ashore. Sometimes, Nik would join in, and grab the other end for a cruise back to land. After a quick shake at the shoreline, Bodie quivered with anticipation, begging for one more launch of the stick.

Sometimes, we just couldn't get him out of the icy waters, no matter what we did. We'd pack up our things from lunch and start down the trail. Bodie would stand and watch, perplexed at our departure, despite his shivers in the cool Sierra afternoon. Even after the hike back to the trailhead, he shivered, and I'd wrap his lean, hard body in a wool shirt to warm him. Of course, Nik was dry and toasty, as we headed home for supper.

Bodie grew, and everything about him got longer—his legs, his body and even his tail, now draped with silky, shimmering fur. When he bounded through the underbrush, we could see the tip of his flag above the sage, waving wildly in his pursuit of a scent or a squirrel.

Whether on backpacks or day hikes, we tried to include at least one swim a day for Bodie. High mountain lakes, nestled in glacial cirques, drew fishermen as well as hikers. Occasionally, we'd have to divert Bodie's attention, so he wouldn't spook the fish and annoy the rod casters. On one outing, we trotted around a small lake, and he slipped past me on the trail, brushing his silvery plume across my bare thigh. Suddenly, I felt something sharp in my flesh. I looked down to see an old rusty fishhook embedded in my leg, just above my knee. "Walter, look! I think Bodie just hooked me."

Our water-loving boy must have snagged a hook discarded by a careless fisherman, and implanted it in my leg with a carefree, happy wag of his tail.

"Not a problem," Walter said and surveyed the situation. "I've seen people remove hooks before. I can do that for you."

"Not on your life! It's rusty and barbed!" We hiked out to the car and made a visit to the emergency room at Mammoth Lakes Hospital.

"Ever seen anything like this?" I joked with the physician on duty. "Oh, yeah, just a few times," he said, and injected the site with Novocain before he removed the hook, and concluded my treatment with a tetanus shot. "But usually, one fisherman hooks another. I've never seen a dog who could do this."

On one of Bodie's first backpacking trips with us, he must have done ten, maybe fifteen, miles the first day. He couldn't take it all in fast enough, but heaven knows he tried. Nikki, of course, was content to cover just as many miles as we did, and arrived at camp tired and happy to curl up by the campfire. But as soon as we set up the tent and spread out our sleeping bags, Bodie slumped inside and collapsed into the sleep of the dead. I had to physically rouse him, and deliver his dinner to him. Exhausted, he ate, then fell back asleep, and didn't move again until dawn. Refreshed and ready to roll, he rocketed off on another day of adventures.

Bodie greeted each season in the Sierras with gusto. He swam and hiked in summer, flashed through fall colors in autumn, and bounded into winter snowdrifts. He even enjoyed the spring ice melt. On an early season hike to Horseshoe Lake above Mammoth, he couldn't wait to plunge into slushy waters still topped by great floating pads of thick ice. He forged ahead through barely thawed water, intent on climbing aboard one of these remnants of winter. Walter and I stood ashore and shivered, then we began to call him back. The more we called, the farther he swam. Worried that one of us would have to brave the icy deep, our entreaties became louder and more frantic.

"He could get stuck under one of them and never get out!" I yelled. Walter began to pull off his Sorels and socks, and prepared to rescue Blond Boy. Suddenly, Bodie turned to look at us as if he hadn't heard a single bleating cry from shore. "Oh, you're over there," he seemed to say. "I'm on my way." Walter heaved the biggest sigh of relief and pulled his boots back on. We leaped aside to let Bodie shake frosty water from his coat.

Nik stood right next to us during this whole scene. But just the day before, the apparently perfect Little Miss had demonstrated a bit of mischief herself. We sauntered through a wide meadow and around several frozen ponds when Nik began to trot out onto the middle of a pond that just a moment before had supported several large, fat geese, preening their feathers. Lured by the scent of their droppings, Nikki headed for the Mother Lode. No entreaties from us could deter her from her mission. Once in the center, Nik flung herself into the fragrant mass and began to roll with great delight, from side to side, then up, then back down. She looked like she was smiling, assured we wouldn't venture onto the ice. Once finished, she ambled back to us, and just as surely into the shower later in the day to be relieved of the pungent odor. Always a lady, but still a dog.

While Nikki never seemed to see the point in a game of fetch, Bodie was obsessed and would play until the dark of night descended or the pitcher's arm fell off, whichever came first. He bolted through the brush in the woods to find an errant throw, sped across expanses of green lawn in parks to scoop up the toss, and leaped toward the heavens to shag a sky ball. Tongue lolling and lungs heaving, he rushed back to us for the next round. If we hesitated at all, he dropped into play bow position, head lowered, rump in the air, and flapped his jaws together in excited anticipation. He continued this laughable display until we tossed the next ball. We dubbed it his "happy clap" and often had to explain it to curious observers.

Bodie grew and matured, but retained the joyful exuberance of his youth well into adulthood. And he became a surprisingly good therapy dog.

Bodie's Prime

Bodie's strong suit at the hospital was humor. His lanky build and ever-present grin made people smile just to look at him. He was a welcome focus for families, who struggled in waiting rooms to pass the time, while their loved ones underwent surgery. All he needed to hear was, "Look, Mom. It's a dog!" from an excited youngster, and he was on his way to brighten the day. Parents always looked relieved when we could offer distraction and a bit of comfort to their children.

Bodie was a hit in pediatrics. With his flexible, supple gait and big tail, he sometimes looked like he had many extra joints in his long body. Kids, parents, nurses and doctors all welcomed him to the unit and exclaimed over his beautiful color, friendly face, big brown eyes and happy disposition. While he didn't have Nikki's tenderness in approaching people, he did have a "hail fellow well met" style that seemed to encourage people not to take things so seriously. Bo's philosophy was why frown when you can smile instead? Nik was a dog you could tell your troubles to, but Bodie was the one to party with.

One patient in particular seemed to understand that truth. Chuck was a youngster all too familiar with the medical world. He'd endured several hospitalizations and had become an introverted, quiet child. There was little the staff could do to bring him out of himself or get him to engage with others. That is, until the dogs arrived.

After one of our early visits with Chuck, Bodie and I said our farewells and left his room. I paused to deposit a bed sheet and hand towel in the linen closet, when this once shy boy suddenly serenaded us. "I feel good!" he crooned. "Like I knew that I would!" he continued, belting out the James Brown classic. Nurses laughed and crowded around his door, enjoying Chuck's air guitar and the joyful outburst that Bodie must have elicited. From that point on, Chuck became a regular on our rounds, and we certainly missed him when he got to go home for good.

Bodie seemed comfortable in most situations at the hospital, except for those that required gentle, slow movements or extra care around a patient's wounds or medical equipment. A bounder at heart, Bodie could leap atop any bed with ease, but I limited the occasions he could do this. Only when I was assured the patient's injuries were encased in a solid plaster cast did he enjoy bed privileges. One woman was thrilled to have a visit. She explained that her leg was in a cast after her own big, strong dog had broken it when he ran into her. Her dog had lurched in greeting, and collided with her tibia. She landed in surgery for repairs.

Bodie's skills were more suited to patients in wheelchairs, who could just drape an arm across his shoulders to enjoy his ear-to-ear grin, almost at their eye level. He always found someone in the rehab garden to share sunshine with, or a family member to visit, while a patient received treatment.

More than anything, Bodie brought a sense of normalcy into a very abnormal environment. He brought the proverbial breath of fresh air and a wag of his tail to everyone he met.

After we commuted for years across L.A., from our coastal home inland to work, Walter and I decided to move, since we both worked in Pasadena. Leaving the Palisades after twenty years was hard, but we were fortunate to find a beautiful home that overlooked a wild canyon in the foothills of Arcadia. A huge plus, especially from Bodie's point of view, was the azure swimming pool right off the deck. Now he could indulge his passion for water without the five-hour drive to the Sierras. And he loved it.

Bodie launched into the water from any deck that surrounded it, and dove after tennis balls and any other toys tossed into his domain. But we soon learned to be careful with our throws, because he had such a wide dive that he could hurt himself had we not been attentive. Why walk down the steps, when you can fly through the air? He seemed to say.

Nikki liked to swim, once we taught her how at a Mammoth lake. She took careful, deliberate steps from the shore and had to be coaxed into deeper water ever so gently, cheered by friends, and supported by Walter, so she could begin to find her dog paddle. The first few forays were tentative, but she gained confidence and began to swim in little circles. At home, we taught her where the steps in the pool were, and she used them every time, stepping in and walking out when she finished her swim.

With other golden and Labrador retrievers in our circle of friends and colleagues from the hospital, it was inevitable that our yard and pool became a gathering place. Many a summer afternoon, Walter returned home from work to find cars lined up on the street in front of the house and gales of laughter rising from the yard. Three or four and even as many as eight dogs and their people frolicked in the water and lounged on the deck above the canyon. The dogs, of course, could swim for hours, until we pulled them out to dry before they headed home. The pool filter sometimes choked on all the golden fur that floated on the surface. Gallons of water drained from the pool when dogs dove, splashed and shook. Toys were lost and found, balls bobbed across the waves, and everyone enjoyed a rowdy good time with wet dogs. What could be more fun than a gaggle of goldens and a pool of water?

We treasured the canyon behind our house. Originally called Wilderness Park, during our years in Arcadia, it became an official wilderness preserve. Admission was limited to certain days of the week and certain hours. For much of the time, it was true wilderness, roamed by deer, bears, coyotes, families of quail and other indigenous species. Despite the proximity to civilization, it had been untouched by fire and grew thick stands of eucalyptus, sycamore, scrub oak and sumac.

A year-round stream provided water for the residents, and also lured Bodie on our walks. Once past the paved parking lot and on one of the dirt roads or trails, we let Nik and Bodie off leash to enjoy their outings. Nik, of course, stayed right with us. Bodie always dashed off to the stream, but came when called. We walked as often as we could, since our home was just a few doors down from the park entrance.

Every season offered something new, even in southern California. During El Nino winters, we watched our little stream swell to historic proportions, and we could hear boulders bash against each other from the force of the water that hurtled them along.

Before moving here, I investigated the presence of rattle-snakes. As dry as the area is, they can be found in many foot-hill regions. I asked local residents and experts, and was assured that our property could be snake-proofed with re-taining walls and small wire mesh. We did so, but still found one in back by the bedroom steps, another in the garage, and a third on the side of the house. Walter bravely dispatched two of them, and captured another for pick up by the local animal control officer. We redoubled our efforts, and re-mained vigilant.

It was a pleasure to be only fifteen minutes from the hospital. I could bring dogs with me, and return home at noon. Walter and I carpooled, since his office was just a few minutes from mine. I'm sure he was the only executive in his company who drove to work with a couple of dogs.

With the move, we recaptured hours and hours of time once lost to crushing freeway commutes. We enjoyed the pool almost as much as the dogs, and gave thanks that we'd found a spot in L.A. so close to the wilderness that we loved. Life settled into a peaceful routine, with satisfying work, soul-enriching trips to Mammoth, and my first horse.

Welcome and Farewell

When I graduated from college, my first roommate suggested we learn to do something we'd never done before. Without a lot of consideration, we settled on horseback riding, since our apartment was near Griffith Park and many stables.

We took lessons, I loved it, she didn't, and I was left with a new hobby, but no way to pursue it. Years passed and a new friend in the PAT program invited me to ride with her. Finally, horses were back in my life.

More lessons and hours of just hanging out at the stable rekindled this love, and led me to purchase my first horse, an Icelandic gelding named Neisti. Icelandics at that time were what Walter called a cult horse with only eight hundred in the U.S. They were short and stout, beloved by their owners and advocates, and the source of some derision by people who couldn't believe these sturdy little beasts could offer such an enjoyable ride.

But I was in love and delighted with my renewed passion. I worked part-time at the hospital and also did medical transcription in an orthopedic surgeon's office. This left me with a somewhat flexible schedule and time to ride. It was the perfect balance of work and play, and a wonderful use of my newfound time.

On an unusually warm Sunday in April, Walter and I decided to walk the dogs in the cooler morning, and then drive to the stable to visit Neisti. We leashed up Nik and Bodie and arrived at Wilderness Park shortly after it opened. We took off on our usual trail, and the dogs trotted off leash at our sides. Bodie made a dash for the stream and then rejoined us just a bit down the road. After a half hour or so, we turned for home and commented on how hot it was. I thought the dogs would enjoy a swim and we planned to let them have a dip before we left for the barn.

Bodie peeled off for the stream again, but didn't return. I called and called again, and saw him struggle up through the low brush. Something wasn't right. He panted heavily, staggered a bit, and then I saw the two small marks on the side of his head.

"Walter, I think he's been bitten," I said, my heart starting to race. "You get him up to the road, and I'll run home for the car."

Everything for the next hour seemed to move in slow motion. I couldn't run fast enough up to the house to bring the car down. Walter loaded Bodie in the back. I pleaded for him to drive faster, while I breathed into Bodie's nose and mouth. The emergency veterinary hospital wanted information I didn't seem to have. Bodie couldn't breathe. They took him in back and sent us home.

"I'm so frightened," I said softly. We drove home, my hands shaking and my heart despairing.

We had no sooner walked in the front door than the phone rang. Yes, they wanted us to come back right away.

More painful slow motion—walk, drive, think. I can't. We returned to the hospital to receive the news.

"We did everything we could," the vet tech said. "He did seem like such a lovely dog," I heard through a thick fog. "Would you like to see him?"

Resting on his side, the artificial airway still in his throat, Bo was now still. I knelt next to him, stroked his silver sides, cradled each and every foot that once flew across the earth and transported him into the wilderness he so loved. I clipped a handful of silver fur from his great flag tail. I said goodbye.

Scarcely able to walk or breathe, we left the hospital. Stunned and shocked by this tragic loss, we needed to do something. We drove to the stable and I stood by Neisti, stroking his neck. I fed him carrots. I could hardly understand how the joy of this new life becoming part of mine was now so tempered by the heart-wrenching loss of another. It must be balance, or the circle or the grand plan. I didn't know. I only ached that deep, deep ache of loss that empties your soul.

Tucker

The Countess had lost her Cowboy.

Nikki tried to fill the void for all of us. The next few days she worked to occupy that huge, gaping space that death leaves. She was everywhere—she smiled, cajoled, comforted and cared. It was hard to watch Nik assume the role of care-taker for both Walter and me.

Then, she crashed, too. One morning, while we dressed for work, she heaved a huge sigh, stepped onto Bodie's bed, settled down, and turned her face to the wall. She was exhausted and missed her buddy as much as we did. We hugged her and cried and told her it was okay to be sad with us. Together we'd all regain our equilibrium.

It took some time. Everyone at the hospital was kind and sensitive and understood my loss. But conducting the next PAT meeting was one of the hardest things I've ever had to do.

From the start of the program, we banded together to mourn the death of any of our partners. There hadn't been many losses, but each was hard, because it touched so many people, even beyond our close-knit group. With the guidance of one of our social workers, I conducted memorial services for each lost dog. We shared our remembrances, cried for our loss, and gave thanks for the joy and experiences we'd shared.

Now, it was my turn. I'd lead the group in memory of my own, dear Bodie. And together we'd honor his life.

It was painful, funny—he was certainly worthy of some good stories—tender, comforting and healing. I brought pictures of Bodie, cavorting through his favorite woods in Mammoth and on the outskirts of Yosemite. One of those fit perfectly in a picture frame I received as a gift. It showed Bodie moving away from the camera, toward the woods, his tail flying through autumn colors, his silver coat aglow. It still sits on a table next to the den sofa.

We talked about the Rainbow Bridge and shared its comforting message.

Just this side of heaven is a place called Rainbow Bridge. When an animal dies that has been especially close to someone here, that pet goes to Rainbow Bridge. There are meadows and hills for all of our special friends, so they can run and play together. There is plenty of food, water and sunshine and our friends are warm and comfortable.

All the animals who had been ill and old are restored to health and vigor; those who were hurt or maimed are made whole and strong again, just as we remember them in our dreams of days and times gone by. The animals are happy and content, except for one small thing: they each miss someone very special to them, who had to be left behind.

They all run and play together, but the day comes

when one suddenly stops and looks into the distance. His bright eyes are intent; his eager body quivers. Suddenly, he begins to run from the group, flying over the green grass, his legs carrying him faster and faster.

You have been spotted, and when you and your special friend finally meet, you cling together in joyous reunion, never to be parted again. The happy kisses rain upon your face; your hands again caress the beloved head, and you look once more into the trusting eyes of your pet, so long gone from your life, but never absent from your heart.

Then you cross Rainbow Bridge together.

— Author Unknown

Friends said farewell to Bodie. I said God must have needed his special spirit somewhere else.

Time passed. Our hearts began to heal. Nikki resumed her rounds at the hospital, and our lives moved on. But the empty space remained, and we knew we were ready for the next golden.

Once again, I connected with the local rescue organizations and put out the word. We needed a sweet, even-tempered dog that could pass muster with Nikki. We took her with us and looked at several candidates. Murray stole her heart.

At the Carson Animal Shelter, we met LaVonne Rodstein, head of SPARE (Save Pound Animals Through Rescue and Education). While her organization rescues all breeds, she's partial to goldens, with five of them in her own life. She thought she might have a dog we'd like.

We met several dogs that all seemed nice, and one that was quite sick that we later learned had to be euthanized.

The kennel was clean, appeared to be well run, and we hoped to find a good match. While we talked and looked at dogs, LaVonne cocked her head to one side and said, "I still have one more dog to show you." She led us toward the trailer where the shelter's caretaker lived.

She brought forth a big, red boy and introduced us to Murray. "We think he's special, so we don't show him to everyone. But I think you might be the right family," LaVonne said.

Murray lumbered toward us, broad and big-boned with the uncoordinated gait of an adolescent. Nik took one look and began to twirl her tail in circles, like a helicopter rotor. "Oh, that's a very good sign!" I exclaimed. "She does that when she's happy." The two dogs sniffed and snuffled around each other, and seemed contented with what they found. So were we.

His first owners had relinquished Murray to the shelter several months earlier. We never learned the real reason, except possibly that the wife had too much on her plate with young children. Now ten months old, Murray had lived happily with the caretaker, but they all knew that he needed to have his own home.

LaVonne arranged for him to be neutered the next day, and we arrived to pick him up the following morning. We planned to attend a celebration for a friend's daughter for her college graduation, and Murray and Nikki were invited. We gathered up our new family member and drove to a garden party. On a lovely late spring day, we walked in with our two goldens. Nikki knew some of the people, and would know the rest shortly. She proceeded to work the crowd and make herself at home.

I swear that Murray looked at the gathering, smiled with

great delight, and said to himself "It's a party. I just love parties!" and moved right in.

Tall as he was, I had to supervise his greetings, so they didn't include helping himself to guests' food off plates on their laps. He puttered around the garden, met the hosts' golden, and thoroughly enjoyed himself. Perhaps he thought it was his own welcome home party.

"I don't think Murray suits him," I observed the next day. "Let's come up with a new name." Walter agreed, and the search began. We tried out all kinds of options, to find a big name for our big boy. Tucker finally fit, and Tucker he became.

Eager to introduce him to our favorite trails in Mammoth, we took him with us two weeks later. We thought he'd be happy to explore the wilderness. We were surprised by his reaction.

He started up a modest trail for a short several mile hike, but stopped frequently to rest in the shade. He wagged his tail, greeted everyone going up or down past his resting spot, and then resumed his walk with us, only to pause a few yards further on. "I think he's a wuss," Walter lamented, missing his ever-reliable hiking partner, Bodie. "Maybe we don't have the right dog for the things we like to do."

Maybe he's hot. Maybe it's the altitude. We made excuses for his lack of enthusiasm for the outdoors.

We were both crestfallen. Although he seemed happy, Tucker really did appear to be a couch potato. Maybe there was some physical issue. I had to get him checked out.

"I want you to take him right over to Animal Specialty Group," Dr. Lippincott said, as he explained what the x-rays showed. "Tucker has hip dysplasia, and they're the right people to help him now."

Shaken by this diagnosis, just one month after Tuck had joined our family, I made the appointment and enlisted Walter to come, too. When we arrived with our boy, the vet confirmed the diagnosis.

"Yes, he has bilateral dysplasia, and will need TPO surgery," Dr. Bilbrey informed us. "And because he's almost one year of age, we'll need to do it soon. Otherwise, the joints will be too badly damaged for anything except total hip replacements."

Triple pelvic osteotomy, he explained, reshapes the hip joint, to give it enough curve to hold the head of the femur in place. He demonstrated how Tucker's hind legs could slip easily in and out of alignment. Pins and plates would hold the reshaped acetabulum in place while he healed. Dr. Wendelberg, an associate of Dr. Bilbrey, confirmed the diagnosis and said he could do the surgery.

Stunned, Walter and I got in our separate cars—he to go back to work and me to take Tucker home. The extent of the surgery and the cost left us both reeling. Suddenly, I had a new perspective. I picked up my cell phone and rang Walter in his car. "If he lives to be ten, that's only a buck a day," I announced hopefully. "I think we should do it." We loved him and there really was no other option.

A week later, I delivered Tucker for his surgery. I awaited word later that day, but was startled when the hospital called mid-morning. "We can't do the surgery today. When we shaved him, we found an extensive skin infection, probably from fleas at the shelter. You'll have to treat him with antibiotics for two weeks and then we can try again."

Now we were about to bump up against that one-year

mark and would have to hope for the best. Tuck came home, shaved from his mid-torso down to his tail, which made him look like a lion. Emotionally prepared for surgery, we now had to ramp down, drop back, and wait two more weeks.

Surgery went well. But on the third day post-op, when I went to visit him, he just didn't seem right. I explained my observation to the staff and went home to receive the doctor's assessment.

At 8 PM, Dr. Wendelberg called. "I agree with you that Tucker's not right," he said. "I think he's depressed. If you can deal with everything, I want him to go home sooner, so he can begin to heal with you."

The next day, I arrived to bring him home. Since both hips had been rebuilt and he couldn't bear any weight on his hind legs, he had to be carried everywhere. A heavy towel worked as a sling, so I could take him up and down steps to the yard. A stellar patient, he began to recover quickly and regain his strength. Once home, his spirits never flagged. And Nik was an attentive partner throughout.

Eight weeks later, with a clean bill of health from his doctor, we re-introduced Tucker to Mammoth trails. This time, he took the wilderness by storm, tackled every trail with joy, and went the distance without hesitation. We took him on our favorite hikes and he never flagged, not once.

If I look closely at photos taken on that trip, I can almost see the line where his coat had been shaved for the surgery. Miraculously, his fur grew back, his hips mended, and he was better than new. What a testament to the skills of our veterinary surgeons and to Tucker's cheerful outlook on life. Where we humans receive a diagnosis and then brood and ruminate on it, our animal friends just take each day as it comes and let nature heal their wounds.

The Message

A fall trip to Yellowstone is one of our favorite adventures. Few crowds, intense colors and active wildlife reward autumn visitors. Nik and Tuck were settled in their life together, and we left them in the capable hands of a good friend, who would house sit for us.

After a number of visits to the park, we knew our favorite spots—the hotels and cabins we preferred, good trails to see animals, and best wildlife watching from the road. We spent several days on the outskirts and perimeter of the park and then ventured to the interior. Late afternoons and evenings spent in the grand sitting room at the Lake Yellowstone Hotel always highlight any trip. Opened in 1891, the two-story structure stretches along a bluff that overlooks the second largest high altitude fresh-water lake in the world. Tall white pillars adorn the original entrance of the iconoclastic yellow building. Views across the vast and sometimes storm-tossed lake contrast with the comfort of the room and soft melodies from the baby grand piano. Guests gather to sip wine, share adventures of the day, or read in quiet corners.

But the view into the heart of the park always draws gazes outside the warmth of the room.

Summer artists in residence may be at work in the nearby lobby. Questions in foreign languages mingle with the English answers. Families, couples and singles seem to blend comfortably, bound by their awe and appreciation for this special place.

After a contented evening of these pleasures, we settled into our room and soon slept. Around midnight, I stirred, unclear what had awakened me. I stared at the ceiling, listening, but heard only Walter's rhythmic breathing next to me.

I slipped out of bed and went into the bathroom. We'd left the small window open, for the fresh night air. I put my elbows on the sill and listened, my chin in my hands. Darkness concealed this remote and exquisite world.

Suddenly, I heard it, as clearly as anything I've ever heard in my life. A wolf howled somewhere across the lake. And again. And one last time.

Transfixed, I didn't dare to move or breathe for fear I'd break the spell. The sound hung in the air, like smoke rising from a campfire.

It was Bodie. He wanted me to know he was fine, free as any creature on earth. Free to roam and roam and roam. God had indeed needed him somewhere else, and this was it.

Tears trickled down my cheeks. I gave thanks, for the message, for his life, and for this gift of knowing.

Born of a union of wind and water, Bo always coursed through the forests like a native child. He could smell water a mile away and swim to tooth-chattering and bone-rattling exhaustion. Poised still and erect in winter snow, he stared into the distance as if divining his next life. Now, here he was, a perfect match of soul and spirit, dressed as wolf.

Sophie

By now, Nikki was middle-aged and in her prime at the hospital. She could meet any situation and handle it with her customary charm and sensitivity. She became a role model for new dogs in the program, and helped to train many of the freshman teams. They shadowed us through the halls, into patient rooms and waiting areas. Together we taught classes, workshops and continuing education courses for health care professionals. If ever there was a pro, it was Nikki.

My dream of taking my dog to work had become reality, and I was grateful for this privilege every single day. I fielded numerous inquiries from across the country and around the world, as other therapists sought the key to introducing this special modality in their settings. It was apparent that this golden girl could touch lives outside our hospital, because the things we learned together and the doors we opened would also benefit patients in Connecticut and Israel, as well as those across town.

With such a skilled co-therapist by my side, I wasn't compelled to train Tucker for the job. Laid back and congenial as he was, I didn't feel that he was interested in having a job. Nik was born to do the work, but I wasn't sure Tucker was.

But Tucker and Bodie had brought another welcome dimension into our lives. Both boys loved the outdoors and kept us constantly planning trips that enriched us all. They pulled us deeper into the wilderness and let us see it through their eyes.

Tucker was still a young dog and liked to play. But since Nik didn't always reciprocate, I began to consider a younger playmate for him.

Walter wasn't convinced. "We already have two big dogs, and we like to travel with them. How would we do that with three?"

"Nikki really isn't a dog," I said. "She has such a grounded sensibility about her. It's almost like having another person along."

Still skeptical, but probably knowing I was headed down this path anyway, Walter sat back to see what would happen. The next golden was already half way into our home, and he knew it.

Once again, I opened doors to look for a new family member. At the same time, Maggie, one of the PAT co-founders, was also on the lookout for a new dog, so we shared information and collaborated in the search.

When I didn't find an appropriate young adult rescue dog, I turned to local breeders. A woman in Riverside had two dogs that Maggie and I thought might be worth seeing. On a bright spring day, we caravanned out to the Inland Empire with our current dogs to meet the candidates.

Rolling green grass and huge shade trees sheltered the rural kennel. Two very blonde dogs rushed down the hill to the gate to welcome us. Aunt and niece, they obviously shared some genetic history, but were also different. Maddie was heavier-boned, lower to the ground and a stockier dog.

Sarah was slighter, quite trim and very fleet of foot. She had a wonderful, wide grin. I turned to Maggie and said, "Well, that's all I need to see!" We opened the gate and walked in to learn more about these beautiful girls.

Since Sarah was intended to be Tucker's playmate, I was eager to see his reaction. I turned to look at him, but he gazed off into the distance, distracted. Glassy eyed, he stared in the direction of the kennel, and huge, long, gobby drools dripped from his jowls. Concerned that he'd picked up something toxic, I asked the breeder what was going on.

"Oh, I have a bitch in season," she said. Apparently, Tucker already was aware of that fact, but had forgotten he was no longer an eligible bachelor. During our entire visit there, he never regained his senses, and scarcely looked at Sarah. It would be up to me to assess her appropriateness as his companion. He'd have to accept my judgment.

Meanwhile, Nikki took all this in with her usual aplomb, while we asked about the two young dogs.

Maddie had been shown a few times, but wasn't likely to be a champion. She'd been set aside in favor of other more successful show ring prospects, and needed a home of her own. Maggie thought she'd make a lovely therapy dog.

Sarah, on the other hand, had never been shown or bred. Just a year old, she'd spent her entire life in the kennel. Whether she'd been sold and returned, I never learned. She'd obviously been socialized to people, and was allowed to play with the breeder's grandchildren. I fell in love on the spot with her engaging spirit. Walter agreed that she was delightful, and so we became a three-dog household.

Sarah bounced across the wide yard with all of us, but balked when we approached the car. Maybe she was afraid of cars, maybe she'd been sick or had an unpleasant experience in one, I reasoned. We gently loaded her into the Explorer with Nikki and Tucker. Paralyzed with fear for the entire ride home, she flattened herself on the floor of the car, her eyes wide with fright.

Once home, I thought she'd relax, but no. When we lifted her out in the garage, she collapsed again, belly pressed to the ground. The other two dogs trotted into the house, but she lay there, overwhelmed by what might lie ahead. We could barely get her to her feet and coax her into the kitchen. That first day was one of terror and shock for dear Sarah.

Concerned, I phoned the breeder. "Oh, it's just that she's never been in a car or inside a house," she said. "She'll get over it."

I was stunned. When we'd left, the woman shed a few tears and we thought she was really going to miss the two girls. But her lack of commitment to young Sarah and her cavalier attitude toward her predicament shocked me. Apparently, she'd done nothing to nurture this sweet dog's nature or prepare her for a home in the real world. Now, she wanted nothing further to do with the situation, and brushed us off. Although I paid for Sarah, I now considered her another rescued dog. Had we not come along, who knows how long this sweet girl might have languished in the kennel, ignored and neglected?

Our task was obvious: introduce her first to our household and then to the world and help her gain confidence. She had a three-month-old brain inside a year-old body. The exuberance and energy were there, but without any training or experience to help her live comfortably in a home with two people and two other dogs. I had to approach her as I would any young puppy, despite her beautiful full-grown body.

Nikki was patient but firm with her. Tucker wasn't sure what she was all about, since he hadn't noticed her until we got home. His drool and testosterone dried up, and he looked around to see dog number three. How had this happened? He seemed to ask.

Sarah was a sweet name, but I didn't think it fit our youngster. A skilled and patient English setter named Sarah worked at the hospital, and I wanted to reserve that name for her. We stumbled on Sophie one day and it fit her to a T. Besides, when we called for the dogs to come, we could sing out "Sophie Tucker," as if we were channeling the spirit of the famed vaudevillian from the 1930s.

The first few days were a challenge. The blonde whirling dervish never stopped moving. On day two, I returned home from work early, suffering a touch of the flu. The threesome greeted me enthusiastically, but knew something was wrong when I headed straight for the bedroom. Nik and Tuck gently found places alongside me on the king-sized bed. Meanwhile, Sophie leaped and charged in a frenzy all around the three of us, while we huddled in the center of the bed. Grateful that Sophie hadn't yet figured out how to bound onto the bed, I lay there, felt miserable, and wondered how to bring order into chaos.

Sophie carried some very specific phobias with her, too. One day, a serviceman arrived to work on an appliance. Usually happy to meet newcomers, Sophie stopped in her tracks and fear flashed across her eyes. A man in heavy boots must have traumatized her and it took months before she could shed that memory.

One afternoon, shortly after she'd arrived, I was folding towels in the laundry room. When I shook out the first towel, Sophie dropped to the floor and scrambled away from the sound. Did it seem like a gunshot? Or did she think she was going to be struck? This, too, took months to recede from her memory. Both episodes further reinforced my hunch that her kennel hadn't been such a nice place for young dogs. Thankfully, she was now with us.

We managed to show her the ropes of living in our family. I needed to find an obedience class and fast. But when we arrived that first night, she was uncontrollable, and I knew I needed something else. I consulted with the animal behaviorist who volunteered his services to the PAT program.

"What she needs right now is less stimulation, not more," Bill Stavers told me, after he observed Sophie. "She's just spinning with everything that is new in her environment. You need to teach her how to calm down and develop some self-control." *From your lips to God's ears. I hope we can do this.*

"You need to begin by standing quietly with her on a leash. No matter what she does, you remain in place, and let her teach herself how to be still," he said. Sounded like the mountain pose in yoga. Doggie yoga.

For the next week, I set aside time each day to take Sophie outside by herself, on a leash in our backyard. She'd spin and twirl excitedly when I went to a different spot on the grass or deck around the pool. There I stood, while this manic little dog wrapped herself around my legs, tugged and pulled, panted and gagged until—finally—she could take a deep breath and begin to settle. Progress seemed miniscule at first. But little by little, she was able to pull herself together and actually take in the world around us at something less than warp speed.

Exercise was also in Sophie's prescription, and she discovered that she loved to swim. It was an easy way to burn some of that excess energy, so she could focus on other things. We added an obedience class, and she performed well. Anything that involved movement was right up her alley, so heeling, circling and trotting were her strong suits. We continued to work on sit, stay and down, and they came into her repertoire, too.

Graduation day arrived and I was excited to show off her skills. We showed up at the park early and practiced maneuvers flawlessly. She was bright and chipper as always and ready to rock and roll.

Her heeling was exceptional, precisely at my left side and attentive throughout. She made her turns crisply and remained in position. When I jogged, so did she. Her score was perfect. I was thrilled.

Then came the long sit (one full minute) and long down (three interminable minutes). Sophie followed instructions, pinned her bottom to the grass in a flash, and bounded toward me. Zero points on that exercise.

For the down, she hit the deck, looked up at me, smiled her toothy grin, and then galloped across the grass to meet me once again. Zero points.

I was crestfallen. My brilliant, bouncy girl had so mastered the motion, but sidestepped the stationary. Her heart wasn't in it, and it wasn't part of her persona to be away from people or sitting still. She loved to bustle, always in a bit of a hurry, so she wouldn't miss anything or anyone.

But at least she'd gained some manners and found her role in our household. She and Tucker became fast friends and enjoyed each other's company. Nik, as usual, remained in an elevated position, more human than dog, but seemed happy to have them around.

The smallest of our goldens, Sophie somehow managed to acquire the longest nickname. We eased into her name change with Sarah Sophie. We added Puppy Cakes, because she was so gentle and sweet. Her petite size gave rise to Baby Bitkin. But we also dubbed her Pie, short for Sweetie Pie. So, her full name grew to Sarah Sophie Puppy Cakes Baby Bitkin, and we often called her just Pie.

Her athletic skills involved speed—running and swimming. But her eye-mouth coordination fell short, and Walter used to say she caught balls like a girl. She often nosed my knee to beg for treats, especially when I chopped watermelon or cheese at the kitchen counter. Neither Walter nor I could resist her infectious smile and succumbed to her wiles more than once. Nik and Tuck benefited from their sister's skillful soliciting, too, and watermelon chunks were shared all around.

Always lured by the Rocky Mountains, we vacationed in Montana, Wyoming and Colorado. For several years, I'd urged Walter to think seriously about early retirement, so we could find our spot in the West. On each trip, I tried on our small town destinations, as if they were coats. Were the sleeves too long? Did it fit across the shoulders? Did I think we could endure the winters? Was there culture to match the beauty? Could it become our home?

In 1997, we split our trip between Jackson Hole, Wyoming and Durango, Colorado. In addition to hiking, fly fishing, horseback riding and photographing, we thought we'd take a look at these two towns a little more seriously. We started in Jackson and perused the real estate ads, strolled the art galleries, and dined in fine restaurants. One night over dinner with friends, who were Jackson residents, I posed my most pressing question. "Tell us about the winters here. What are they really like?" I asked on this crisp October evening. "Well, last year was a bit more than most," our host answered. "I think we had about six hundred inches of snow."

I paused with my fork in mid air. I wasn't sure I'd heard correctly. "That's over fifty feet of snow!" The California girl in me shivered. I liked winters at Mammoth, where three hundred inches blanketed the mountain, but spring came, summer flourished, and fall lasted well into October. I knew I wasn't cut out for months and months of long, hard and very, very cold winters.

Sobered by that realization, and also by the real estate prices, we traveled south to Durango. Settled at the foot of the rugged San Juan Mountains at 6512 feet, Durango resonated with the cowboy culture of the Southwest. Rugged outdoor enthusiasts populated the streets, along with today's ranchers and local business people. Town buzzed with energy and marked time with the whistles of The Train — the Durango and Silverton Narrow Gauge Railroad. Daily departures allow passengers to travel back in time and up narrow, spectacular Cascade Canyon fifty miles to Silverton. Once a thriving mining and mill town, Silverton now boasts about six hundred year-round residents at 9305 feet. They have big winters; down slope Durango has more modest seasons.

We stayed with an acquaintance from Los Angeles whom I'd met while doing medical transcription. Mariam's husband was an anesthesiologist, and they'd just built a log home in Durango. It was a wonderful opportunity to get to know her better, become acquainted with her dogs, and see the community through the eyes of a new resident.

Walter and I sat on the outdoor patio of The Palace Restaurant adjacent to the train station, and enjoyed a late lunch on a sunny, warm and seductive autumn day. We overheard two women at the table next to us talk about recent winters. I had to interrupt.

"Excuse me. Can you tell us what an average winter is like here?"

"Average is about seventy inches of snow," one woman answered, "but the sun shines all the time and the weather never slows us down. Storms blow in, it snows for a day or two, and then the sun comes out, the roads clear off, and it's just beautiful."

This sounded very promising.

"As long as we're here, we might as well look at a few properties," I suggested to Walter. Of course, that's like going to the shelter just to look at the dogs, but it was time to do some real investigation.

We connected with another California ex-patriot turned Durango real estate agent to explore key areas and learn more about this vibrant town. For several days, we'd driven past a property for sale on our way up and down the valley that leads north out of town toward Silverton. Late one afternoon, as a thunderous storm blew in, we stopped for a look.

Set on nearly ten acres, backed up to national forest, overlooking the valley and the route of the train, it offered mountain and meadow views. Nestled mid-property, the house felt warm and comfortable. I stood at the kitchen window with rain imminent and caught sight of the barn. The fenced paddock was right in view. I'd always dreamed of keeping my horse at home and watching him graze right outside my door. For me, this was a dealmaker.

We returned home to Arcadia and all the excesses of Los Angeles and pondered our next step. Each day, we had the same conversation: "I think we should buy it," one of us would announce over breakfast or dinner. "No, I'm just not sure yet," the other would answer. The next day, the roles reversed. It was almost a game of rock, paper and scissors. One day we both said, "I think we should buy it," so we did.

Moving East into the West

Suddenly, we owned a home in the Rocky Mountains. Our dream verged on reality, and now we had to set many things in motion.

"Boys and girls," I announced to the dogs when we returned home, "we're moving to the mountains!" They swarmed around us, expecting dinner or a romp. Little did they know how our lives would change.

We closed escrow in late October and purchased a bed, two nightstands and a dresser. That plus a few items we'd haul from our place in Mammoth would see us through until we made the final move.

At Christmas that year, we drove across the Mojave Desert, into Flagstaff and through the Navajo reservations of the Southwest. The Explorer was filled with golden dogs, and the U-Haul carried basic household needs. We arrived after nightfall and made the bed, fed the dogs, and slept for the first time in our new home.

The next morning seemed dark, even for December. When I pulled up the shades, a magical scene spread before us. We looked eastward, up the hill to the mountains behind the house, to see everything draped in white, as soft snow continued to fall. The tall pines, stately firs and fluffy mountain junipers were dressed in their Christmas best. I chortled with glee and flung open the door to the upper deck and hillside, and the dogs raced down the stairs into their new world. They ran and rolled and chased each other, then stopped to sniff some amazing scent, shovel their noses through the snow, and paw at the source.

Usually sedate and well mannered, Nikki transformed in the snow. She tucked her little behind under her and ran through the drifts, and spun donuts left and right before she flopped down to make dog angels on her back. Tucker lumbered along, relishing everything so new to him. Sophie became a downhill racer, charging uphill only to turn and tear down the fall line as fast as she could go. This was a whole new experience, and they threw themselves into it with gusto.

While the dogs explored their very own private winter wilderness, we set up housekeeping inside. It didn't take long, since we had very little to work with. But our joy and the dogs' enthusiasm more than filled the air. From the first minute, it felt like home.

A round, green plastic patio table and four matching chairs became our dining set. What it lacked in style, it made up for in flexibility. It fit nicely, with lots of room to spare, in the formal dining room, with a splendid view of our back acres and the mountains. With very little effort, we could shift it into the living room, overlook the valley, and watch the train chug north toward narrow, frosty Cascade Canyon.

Christmas Eve brought a fire to the fireplace, and the ever-festive, if not elegant, red sauce for spaghetti to our green holiday table. My cooking options were pretty limited, with just a few pans and utensils. The dogs were exhausted after trying to take it all in. They'd burrowed in snow, chased a couple of rabbits, left wild and crazy tracks from their explorations, and claimed this wondrous place as their own. Settled in our green plastic chairs before the fire, we stroked their sleeping heads, gave thanks, and counted our abundant blessings.

Still pinching ourselves to make sure this was real, we returned to California. It was time to make a plan and execute it.

As often as we could, we loaded the well-traveled dogs into the Explorer and headed for the place we now called home. Whenever we pulled into the driveway, and I got out of the car to open the chain on the black stock gate, tears spilled from my eyes. I'd never known such a strong pull of place before, and always felt that my spirit was once again whole when I was here. It was easy to connect with land that supported tall conifers rooted to the ground, that nourished bears, elk, deer and rabbits, and that offered roosts and nests for eagles, herons and woodpeckers. The space, the air and the beauty drew me and held me safe. I felt nurtured just being there.

Born and raised in New York City, Walter was making an even more dramatic transition. When he first moved to California, his apartment overlooked a small local boat harbor. After we were married and began to look at real estate, I saw his discomfort when we explored more remote canyons, like Mandeville and Topanga. When we asked a realtor what the chain link cages behind one house were for, Walter blanched at the answer: "The owners used to keep the lions there."

Now, he ventured into the true Old West and would settle on land that had seen homesteaders arrive in horse-drawn wagons and dodge downtown gunfights.

Summer approached, and the prospect of another searing, smoggy and stifling season loomed before me. Walter suggested a plan: I should take the dogs and spend the summer in Durango. He'd come to visit every other weekend, and I could check out our new community, sort of like an advance party. "Perfect!" I said, and started to pack.

After I'd spent virtually every summer of my life in the Los Angeles area and dreamed of the mountains, I was finally here. My country girl heart once trapped in a city girl life was now free to soar and explore, with as much excitement as the dogs. It was heaven.

I read *The Durango Herald* cover to cover every morning, and jumped into local clubs and activities. I hiked with Seniors Outdoors! and learned some of the trails. I attended La Plata Quilters Guild and made quilts for the twin beds in the guest room. I volunteered with Cadence Therapeutic Riding. I photographed the dogs and the wilderness and became a regular at the photo store.

I planned hikes, dinners and explorations for Walter's visits. My travel-weary husband arrived from sea level on Friday nights, his plane sometimes forced to dodge great displays of lightning storms, and we hit the ground running—or at least hiking—on Saturday mornings. The dogs greeted him with glee and took to the trails with us. I drove us home from our high country hikes, while Walter napped in the car to recover in time to enjoy one of Durango's good restaurants that evening. Sunday saw more of the same. Sunday evening, or at dawn on Monday, he flew back to recuperate in the city.

This setting better matched Sophie's and Tucker's spirits, too. They could carouse to their hearts' content on acreage that was also home to many local wild creatures. Rabbits, squirrels and chipmunks provided endless entertainment, whether the dogs chased them outside or were glued to the glass of the French doors to watch from the house. A small herd of deer liked to graze across the upper reaches of our hill, and sprang over the fences. Elk crossed the property, when they moved to and from higher altitude pastures in spring and fall. Early one April morning, the dogs set up a ruckus in the dining room. We wrapped robes about us and shuffled in our slippers to peer up the hill, alongside the excited dogs. Even Nikki was atwitter.

A herd of about thirty elk trudged up the dirt road past our barn and headed for the rock cliffs—wide-antlered bulls mixed with muscular cows and a few yearlings. Entranced by the scene, we quietly opened the French doors and left the agitated dogs to pace behind. We padded uphill and stood next to the paddock, watched and listened to this seasonal rite of spring, while the herd moved toward high summer meadows. The animals struggled up the narrow, rocky game trail, and snorted and puffed with exertion. We heard their hooves strike on loose rocks and knock some off the path. Steam puffed from their nostrils in the chill morning air. Spellbound by their power and grace, we watched until the last white rump ascended the steep slope, crested the ridge, and disappeared from view.

For two years, we remained part-time residents, while we arranged to shed our city skins for real life in the country. We rented the Durango house for a few months to a local family, while they remodeled their home. We made regular pilgrimages to the mountains, ever more certain of our decision.

The dogs traveled happily back and forth with us. Three goldens plus all our gear packed the Explorer, but no one complained. The mountains awaited, with sights, smells and glories to discover.

On one occasion, we traveled like royalty. Given the opportunity to fly on a private jet, we at first demurred, saying we'd have our dogs with us. However, the charter jet company said, "That's no problem at all. Elizabeth Taylor flies with her dogs all the time." After we confirmed that the three big goldies were indeed welcome, we thought, *What a lark!*

When we drove into the small airport, we were directed right onto the tarmac next to the plane. Staff members loaded all our gear on board. Nikki, Sophie and Tucker bounced out and charged up the ramp into the cabin. They sniffed the leather seats, trotted up and down the aisle, greeted the cabin crew, and made themselves right at home.

Walter and I buckled into our seats and held the dogs next to us for takeoff. The jet rumbled down the runway, picked up speed, and lifted off the ground. Tucker panted, uncertain about this new sensation. Sophie grinned and wiggled. Nikki settled back to enjoy the ride. We shared our lunch with them and relished the two-hour flight, a welcome alternative to the two-day drive.

After two weeks in Durango, we returned to the airport for the flight home. We pulled up at the private terminal, to see an even bigger Gulfstream parked outside. "Walter, that can't be our plane," I whispered. "It looks bigger than the United commuter jet sitting at the main terminal."

But it was our plane. Embarrassed by this excess, we reminded the crew that we were only two people and three dogs. They reassured us that we were just part of their schedule that day and welcomed us aboard. The dogs climbed the stairs and settled in like old hands at such luxurious travel. But we warned them that this wasn't going to become our standard mode of transportation.

At twelve going on thirteen, Nikki left rigorous exploration to Sophie and Tucker. But she continued to putter on the hillside, or stroll the front lawn, observing and enjoying—the matriarch at leisure. I'd retired from the hospital, leaving the PAT program in Maggie's capable hands. After ten years, it had achieved national recognition and become a model for other facilities. When I left, forty teams of volunteers and their dogs carried on in our footsteps. The program continues today, a tribute to those first three dogs and their remarkable skills.

While Nik aged, ever so gracefully, her vets and I followed a small distension in her abdomen. At first, no one was alarmed. Blood work and exams in both Durango and Pasadena showed some irregularities, but no one was able to pin down a diagnosis. Nik seemed comfortable, so we adopted a wait and see approach.

Eventually, a more complete examination seemed warranted. We returned to our friends at Animal Specialty Group, where Tucker had been a star patient, and asked their opinion on Nik's condition. Once again, abnormalities were present, but even a needle biopsy wasn't conclusive. Ultrasound showed enlarged organs. The cause could be determined only by exploratory surgery.

Walter and I left the veterinary hospital with Miss Nik that day to ponder the right course for her. After soul searching, we agreed not to subject her to major surgery. The weeks or months that remained for her would be spent in our loving embrace, and we'd treasure every single day together. Her comfort and dignity were more important than possibly gaining a brief extension of her life. We felt the price she'd have to pay in pain and invasive treatments was much too high.

That spring, I wrote from my heart what this beautiful dog meant to me:

One name wasn't enough.

More than any other dog we've had, Nikki seemed to inspire a logbook full of nicknames. NikNik, Nickers, Nicolette, Little Babes, Nickamus, St. Nik. But the best was probably Moose Twickle. God knows where that came from, but Walter started it one day and it stuck. This also gave rise to the verb "to twickle," which was Nikki's slow meander through the yard, in a field, off leash. She's not ready to come in, and we exhort her to "stop twickling and get in here!" She especially likes to do this in Durango in the cold in the snow in the winter. Go figure.

She led me places I never would have dared to go alone.

We began our career together, volunteering at an adult day health center for Alzheimer's patients. I was nervous, startled, self-conscious and uncertain. Nikki was kind, enthusiastic, graceful and centered. She made the visits fun, and I was pleased to see that we could make a difference. I began to think we could do this seriously and started to explore the options. I quit work and began school in recreation therapy — all with the goal of doing animal-assisted therapy.

We never looked back.

From the first day we arrived at Huntington, she was my guide. Her intuition was amazing, her grace enviable, her charm irresistible. I watched in awe as she lifted patients out of their doldrums and left them smiling. What a gift she had. Her generosity was unfailing, as was her blindness to any and all afflictions.

She's always been the best part of me.

When I was tentative, she was enthusiastic. When I was scared, she was courageous. When I was tense, she was relaxed. Whenever anyone needed her, she was there.

She was my guide. She was my teacher. She was my confidant.

Things that were hard for me were easy for her: meeting strangers, being gracious, being open to everything, working in a stressful environment, treating everyone with kindness and openness.

Open — there's the beauty of her soul again. Her eyes have never shut anyone out. Her heart is always true. Her spirit is pure.

It will take me a lifetime to know the lessons she has taught and the kindness she has shown. She always reminds me to step out of my own way, to let things be, to be happy.

She is surely the most remarkable gift to ever come into my life. There will never be another one like her.

She stands alone. I've promised her that she'll always be my Number One Girl. Other female dogs will be part of my life. But none of them will have Nikki's place. When she's gone, we'll retire that number.

For now, she carries the banner of the PAT founding dogs alone. We miss them, her friends and colleagues. But we're so grateful for the years we shared and the pathways we pioneered.

I'm fortunate to write this ode to Nikki while she dozes peacefully at my feet, in her favorite place under my desk. It's a joy to celebrate her life, while she lives in contented retirement. She's eating well, always enjoys the company of others, people and dogs alike, and is just as open and generous as ever. Of course, she sleeps more, exercises less, and needs help to get onto the bed. But she is very much the Nikki I've always known and loved.

We shared a dream. We made a difference. You can't ask for more than that.

Thank you, Nikki. You changed my life. I'll always love you.

May 20, 1998

We spent glorious summer weeks in Durango, all five of us. The two youngsters romped, rolled and reveled in it all. Nikki wandered, contented, napped in the sun, and soaked up all the best in life those precious days.

Back in Arcadia, autumn days slipped away, and so did Nikki's strength. Her spirit remained strong, but I watched for a sign. I asked her to let me know when it was time. I remembered sage advice from a veterinarian I'd known years before, when I asked how I'd know when it was time to consider euthanasia.

"In my experience," he said, "once you ask that question, it might even be just a bit past the right time."

We humans so desperately want to cling to hope, and to our beloved dogs. We can't bear to see them suffer, but can't bear to let them go.

Thanksgiving came and went, and we continued to cherish Nikki's presence. But when we planned for the Christmas trip to Durango, I wasn't certain she could endure the long two-day car trip. A decision loomed before us.

I knew the time I dreaded had arrived. When Nik could no longer stand after relieving herself, and was left to sit in her own puddle, I knew.

I met her devoted veterinarian Peter Lippincott late in the afternoon at his practice. He evaluated all the dogs for the PAT program, but had a soft spot in his heart for the first three goldens, who set the standard for all who would follow.

Everyone was gone except for his receptionist. Together they ushered us into the back room and helped me lift Nikki up to the table. Gracious and kind as always, she extended her paw to greet him. He brushed something from his eye and began to work.

I cradled her beautiful head, told her how much I loved her, and told her it was okay to go. Ever the lady, she gently slipped from this earth to a far, far better place. In the still and darkening light of evening, Peter and I sat together with her. "I'm just not ready to leave," I apologized.

"That's fine," he said.

We talked about PAT and what we'd all achieved together. How splendid the first three dogs had been. What a difference we'd made in people's lives. He stroked her silky fur. "You know, there won't be another one like her," he said, his voice soft.

"We were so lucky," I murmured. Then, I kissed her good-bye.

I sat in the living room, while darkness descended around me. Nikki's collar encircled a single candle that burned brightly. My deep sadness was tempered by knowing what a glorious life she'd lived, and how privileged I'd been to stand by her side, to learn her lessons, and to love her. Walter arrived home, we held each other and cried. It was the end of an era.

The next day, I bumped through life, ran into walls, and waited to hear from Nikki. Bodie's message had been so special; I wondered what Nikki's would be. That afternoon, I walked Sophie and Tucker up the hillside streets in our quiet neighborhood, hoping the air and physical exercise would refresh me. I trudged along with bowed shoulders and heavy heart, and then her message came. It was as clear as those snowy mornings she so enjoyed, bright as a mountain sunrise. And she wasn't alone, either.

I wrote the following to remember every glistening moment of her message, and to memorialize all the other PAT dogs that had already journeyed to the Rainbow Bridge. All their names are real, and I tried to capture a bit of their personalities, as they waited for Nikki at The Bridge.

Welcome Home, Nikki

"Bodie! Booodieee! Boooodieeee!" Sunny called out in the warm afternoon air.

"Where is that guy?" wondered Tara.

"Probably out on the lake. Or maybe down by the river. Oh, I think I saw him in the stream in the meadow." Sunny knew all the watering holes.

"Well, he better hurry up. Someone's coming. Someone he really loves a lot."

"How come you know this before the rest of us do?" asked Chewie, from his full stretched-out-on-his-back and happy-to-be-there pose.

"Because I was the last one down there with our people," Sunny said with a grin. "You remember what it was like when you were first here."

"Booodieee! I'll bet he's off with Monty and Saffie. They love to do all the outdoor stuff together," said Mac. He settled down sedately in the green grass of the meadow.

"But at least they're fast, so I know they won't miss her." Jake appreciated anyone who was fast.

"How do you know it's a her?" asked Tangible, coming in from a romp, with her usual mischievous twinkle.

"Because I just know," answered Jake.

"There they are — finally! I knew they'd make it," said Honey, trotting along the stream toward the group

"So is everybody here?" asked Sunny. "I don't mean everybody, like all our new friends and everything. I mean all the PAT dogs."

"One, two, three, nine — yup, we're all here," pronounced Jake, who did everything fast and often skipped a step or two in the process.

"So, can I be first over the bridge today?" pleaded Sunny. Bodie, Saffie and Monty bounded up, panting and obviously pleased with their run.

"No," said Honey. "Bodie is her brother, so he gets to go first. And Saffie and Monty were her first partners, so they get to go next. And then, me. And then, you, Sunny. And then, everybody else."

"Howdy! What's up, you guys?" Bodie arrived and flopped down in the tall grass, tongue lolling out.

"You got here just in time. I think she's coming today," announced Sunny.

"Really?! Wow—I can't wait to see her. She was my best friend. They called us the Countess and the Cowboy. I guess that makes me the cowboy, huh?" he grinned. He grins a lot.

"How come she's here now?" asked Monty, joining the crowd.

"Because she was sick like I was down there. Something went wrong inside and she just wasn't able to carry on in that body. Her mom is brave like my mom was," said Saffie.

"It seems so hard for our people," Monty said, looking thoughtfully down into the clouds below. "They always cry so much. It makes me sad to see that."

"But you know they'll be okay," said Sunny. "That just means they love us a lot. Really a lot. Really, really a lot."

Bodie joined Monty, Saffie and Sunny, standing tall and long, his plume of a tail ruffled by the warm breeze like a flag. They stood quietly and watched, as the small group of people gathered around Nikki, and their friend Peter took her paw in his hand. He was very sad, too.

"She looks tired," Bodie said, "and sad. This has been a difficult week for her, I think. She tried so hard to stay as long as she could. Her body just couldn't do it any longer. I'm glad mom decided to help her come back up here with us."

"Okay everybody, get ready. She's on her way!" Sunny danced in anticipation.

Bodie started slowly across the bridge. It's the only one there, and the way to connect with their people and their friends. Everywhere else is wide open, free and beautiful.

But then, he couldn't contain himself and he bounded ahead, to be in just the right place when Nikki came through the clouds to find herself face-to-face and nose-to-nose with him. He waited just a heartbeat for her to open her eyes and see him.

"Nikki! Nikki! Oh, Nikki!!" he cried, as he danced around her, finally stopping in front and lying down with a happy clap and a grin as wide as the skies. "Oh, Nikki — come-come-come-come! I love you! We're all here! Look — see?"

Nikki paused to gather herself together, and shook to fluff out her once again full, luxurious and curly golden red coat. Her eyes cleared and she could see forever. Her head rose and she embraced the whole group in a glance. She trotted across the bridge and Bodie danced alongside in joy.

One by one, they all came to greet her, polite, exuberant, sweet, loving and playful. Sniffs, licks, spins and twirls greeted her. She breathed in the beautiful air and the joyful moment and knew she was home.

"I'm so glad to see you all," she said. "I knew you'd be here. But I'm so concerned about my mom. She

93

had such a hard time letting me go," Nikki worried, ever concerned about others.

"I know," said Monty. He came alongside to guide her gently toward the brilliant green meadow. "It's been the same for all of us. But we each had a special way to let our people know that we will still be there, and how well we are here."

"We each sent a special message back in a special way," said Bodie, becoming serious for a moment. "I sent mine when she was in Yellowstone. I did it with a beautiful wolf howl across the lake in the middle of the night. She knew right away it was me, and that I was there for a time. It made her cry, but it was beautiful."

Nikki paused to think a moment. "I want to do it right away," she said. "Christmas is coming, and I want her to know I'm well as soon as possible."

The evening came and all the PAT dogs walked, trotted and played together. They always have so much to share when another one arrives. Nikki received a special welcome and felt very contented. The pain was gone. Peace arrived.

But as they all settled in the meadow together to sleep, she slipped away. She went over by the bridge and looked down. In her house, she saw a single candle burning next to her collar. She saw them cry. She sat by the bridge to decide on her message.

By morning, she knew what to do. She went through the meadow, pausing here and there to collect holly leaves and berries, which she put 'round her neck like a wreath. She breathed in the fragrant and inspiring air and it became gossamer angel wings.

She went to Bodie and shared her plan. Later in the day, they left the others to cross the bridge together. They saw their mom walk Sophie and Tucker up the road, and Nikki and Bodie suddenly began to spin, cavort and dive all around her shoulders. Their joy was almost audible, Nikki's wreath was like a shower of joy from the sky. They played like puppies, sat on her shoulders, sprang into the sky, and twirled among the trees.

They followed her all along the walk. She knew they were there and it made her laugh and cry. It lifted the pain from her heart and let love and joy come in. It let her see peace.

Night fell and winter's chill descended. Their mom settled at the computer to write, weep and heal. Sophie and Tucker lay at her feet. Their dad arrived home and life began to feel good again.

Back in the still, lush meadow, Nikki and Bodie lay side-by-side, quiet together. Stars began to light the sky.

"It was good," said Bodie. "You had a good idea. She liked it a lot."

"And we can be there all the time," said Nikki, staring off into eternity. "I'll never leave her. And now she knows that."

It was love everlasting.

Even in our mountain haven, it was a blue and somber Christmas that year. Sophie and Tucker also seemed quiet. We gathered around the fire, nursed our wounded hearts, and missed our girl.

Glad Dog Ranch

Back in L.A., spring was a time of frenzied activity, as we prepared to leave the city behind and become full-time Durango residents. I assisted my parents in selling their house and divesting thirty-five years' worth of acquired possessions stashed in every cupboard and closet. We helped them settle in a handsome retirement community in Redlands, California. Tally: one house down, two to go.

Next, we began the same process for our own home in Arcadia. Now experienced in making those myriad decisions to sort, clean, sell and donate, I marshaled my energy to accomplish the same for us. The dogs were excited by all the activity, but began to look perplexed, wondering what this was all about. "Don't worry, kids," I explained, wiping grime from my hands and sweat from my brow. "You're gonna love where this is leading."

We took advantage of an early spring to list with our real estate agents. Beautiful weather and the tranquil wilderness canyon that abutted the property helped to generate frequent showings, and we secured a solid offer. Tally: two houses down, one to go.

The listing in Mammoth was a little more problematic. A recent spate of reports about ground tremors, potential earthquakes, and even volcanic eruptions ushered caution into their real estate market. I also think that our karmic reluctance to let go of a place that had brought us—and all our dogs, too—so much joy may have slowed the sale. Our place in Mammoth had let us practice multi-season living in a true mountain environment. In a way, Mammoth had been the training wheels on our life cycle. We learned how to steer, pedal and move through the wilderness with joy, and we cherished those experiences. Letting go was hard, even while we pointed the cycle toward Durango.

But a buyer did arrive for our refuge from the city. We gathered up a few more belongings and said a fond farewell to Mammoth. We'll always treasure our memories of watching Nikki meander through meadows, Bodie plunge into lakes, Tucker first resist and later conquer trails, and Sophie smile through all our days there.

The last few weeks were a blur. We juggled dates, buyers and moving companies to fit all the pieces together. An added complication involved Walter's job. He'd taken a new position just a year earlier. Unfortunately, or perhaps fortunately in the long run, he didn't find the corporate culture of his new company a good fit. Committed to complete several projects before leaving, he couldn't depart with the rest of us as we'd hoped.

Once the van was loaded, we waved to the movers, and all departed for the two-day drive to Durango. Sophie and Tucker bounded into the Explorer, open to adventure and about to be rewarded beyond their wildest imaginations. We arrived on June 22, unloaded our belongings, and began to breathe the fresh air of our new life.

Walter flew back to L.A. and would rejoin us later.

The dogs and I spent the next weeks reveling in this glorious place that we could now, at long last, call home. In between unpacking and tending to the abundant summer gardens, we took walks along the river, climbed some mountain trails, and gamboled through lush meadows of mountain wildflowers.

On a gorgeous Colorado Wednesday, three of my new friends and I took an hour's drive to a renowned nursery and landscaping store in Dolores. We shopped for new additions to our gardens, enjoyed lunch, and browsed the streets of nearby Cortez. At exactly 3:00 PM, standing at a corner waiting for the light to change, I checked my watch. "Ladies," I announced, "Walter is just starting the meeting with his boss. Let's all send him our good thoughts—and hope they don't make him an offer he can't refuse!" Solemnly, we all envisioned Walter in his Brooks Brothers suit, in a high-rise corner office in smoggy downtown L.A., and then waited for my cell phone to ring with the good news. Yes! He could now count down the next two weeks to paradise.

That Saturday morning, Walter met the buyer of his car at the airport, handed over the keys, and boarded the plane for Durango. From the moment his feet hit the ground in Colorado, he never looked back. He hugged the dogs and me in jubilant celebration of all we'd achieved and all that lay ahead of us.

The carved oval sign at the entrance to our property features a picture of Sophie, centered inside curved letters, and set off by pine boughs. We agreed on the name before we ever laid eyes on this beautiful piece of land that would become not only our home, but also our sanctuary. While in Jackson Hole, we'd driven several times past a guest ranch with a sign that said Mad Dog Ranch, with the likeness of an unfriendly dog. We wondered how that served to welcome guests. One afternoon, I said to Walter, "I know what we should call our place: the Glad Dog Ranch! We're always going to have goldens, and they're as happy and glad as dogs can be."

Tucker's likeness is on our letterhead and he and Sophie are on the masthead of *The Glad Dog News, The Not Quite Daily from Durango*. I sent this quarterly newsletter to friends during our first two years here, where I chronicled observations of newcomers, as we became integrated into the splendid community that is Durango.

Of course in real ranchers' terms, our little ten-acre parcel hardly qualifies as a ranch, but to former city dwellers, it's a wide expanse, and I suppose could support a whole passel of retrievers. I still get asked if we breed, show and train. I say no, we don't breed, and while I keep trying to train and do go to competitions, we're only moderately successful at that. Working with our two current active, energetic and opinionated young dogs keeps me humble.

We're fortunate that five of our six dogs have trod our land, lounged on the decks, and blessed this house with their spirits. Photos show Nikki sitting amid the summer flowers and grasses on the hill. Walter snapped me with Nik, Sophie and Tucker, when we paused during a romp just at the foot of the cliffs. A favorite photo shows a contented Sophie lying in a small stream, next to Walter, while he casts a fly in the water. Winter scenes show our current dogs, capturing Daisy's athleticism and Chatter's happy grin in deep powder. Only Bodie, perhaps the dog most connected to the wilderness, missed the chance to know this place.

When we arrived here as new full-time residents in the summer of 1999, Sophie and Tucker settled in well. Easy going by nature, and happy just to greet each day with a romp on our hillside, they took every event, guest and adventure in stride.

If Sophie could have had one wish, it would have been to bring the swimming pool with her. We tried to meet her needs here with hikes alongside streams and rivers, or to snow-fed lakes in the high country. Toward the end of summer, when some sources dried to a trickle, she could find comfort—and relief on warm days—in mud. These weren't just small puddles left after brief summer thunderstorms. These were formerly swimmable ponds, now reduced to five or six inches of thick, black ooze. Stream crossings on trails had become, in Sophie's mind, inviting, soothing wallows.

Where Bodie raced through forests and across meadows to find lakes for some true swimming, Sophie was willing to settle for a semblance of a swim. Actually, I think she was more interested in cooling off. At home, she sometimes settled for sitting in her oversized water bowl. On hikes, she'd speed down a trail until she found a dark wet bog and settle herself in the middle with a sigh of contentment. With a big smile, she slapped her tail in the slime, and waited to greet us, ecstatic over her discovery. We rounded the bend to see her silver-white coat now the color of tar. We soon learned to carry a huge supply of old towels—the bigger, the better—in the back of the Explorer. Otherwise, she would have had a very long hike home.

Tucker traveled the trails with the more mature and contented demeanor of someone who knew his limits. Sure, he could dash off in pursuit of a ground squirrel, but he was more likely to jog at our heels than sprint ahead. His re-built hips never seemed to cause him pain, and it always gave us pleasure to see him able to enjoy the wilderness. He was on his way to realizing my prophecy of being the "Buck a Day Dog," amortizing the cost of his surgery over at least ten years of happy days in our family.

Now the patriarch of the pack, Tucker became a benevolent statesman. A down- to-earth dog, without pretense, he lived each day true to his sweet nature. Oversized for the breed, his big beautiful head could just reach table height, and he could sweep his long tongue across the edge of any unattended plate. Relaxed and happy by nature, Tuck waggled his head from side to side, and greeted everyone with a gentle, "Woo woo!"

When friends from L.A. arrived, especially those from the PAT program who brought their dogs with them, Sophie and Tucker entertained their guests like royalty. The arrivals and welcomes were usually raucous affairs, with lots of hugs, dog wiggles, occasional howls of joy and unending attention. Sophie thought it wonderful entertainment to retrieve everyone's shoes from the porch or deck or even guest rooms and redistribute them throughout the house and the yard. Despite warnings to every overnight guest to close suitcases or bedroom doors, Sophie could strike at will.

She especially liked Jane's underwear. Nearly every morning of a week's visit, Sophie greeted us in the dining room at breakfast with a different article from Jane's collection. This always elicited an embarrassed outburst of, "Oh, no! Sophie!" and Jane had to gather up her unmentionables and give Sophie a hug. No wonder the little lass continued her raids.

Tucker, the party animal, was the unquestioned host of evening gatherings. He never lost his enthusiasm for perusing a party, and cadging a snack or two, some attention and many exclamations over his beautiful head and sweet temperament.

Sophie had practiced her thievery on us. Our shoes were strewn all over the yard, no matter the season. If we left them on the floor, they were hers to corral and re-distribute. She also loved to pick selected bits of treasure from Walter's office trashcan and parade in front of us and our guests with candy wrappers, shopping receipts or scrap paper. Mind you, she didn't want you to have them, just to notice her charms and exclaim over her clever tactics.

Small, slim and trim, Sophie could follow other creatures under the back deck that was set about twelve inches above the ground, next to the grass. One afternoon, she appeared to have exceeded even her limits.

"Walter, where's Sophie?"

"I don't know—somewhere out here. Sophie!"

Thump, thump, thump.

"I hear her tail, but I don't see her."

Thump, thump, thump.

I tracked the thumps and realized that she was nestled deep beneath the deck.

"Come on, sweetie, come on out this side. You got in there, now come on out."

She wouldn't—or couldn't—budge. I feared that she'd gotten her collar snagged on a nail and was stuck. I convinced Walter that we had to do something, so he fetched his circular table saw and began to cut into the deck to free Pie.

Just when we were about to lift out several lengths of sawn decking, Sophie wriggled free and surprised us from behind. Her grin said it all—what a fun game!

The dogs made friends with other canines. Their favorites were Mariam's pack of border collies. At any given time, she probably had four to six underfoot at her home just up the road from us. Some were hers and a steady stream boarded with her, while friends were out of town. No matter the number, they all seemed to fit in the back of Mariam's Toyota 4 Runner. "Load up!" Mariam would sing out, and a wave of black and white fur on feet surged into the back of the vehicle. Sometimes, they tumbled out in our yard for a romp. Sometimes, they got to ride into town and, on a very good day, Mariam drove through the local Dairy Queen on Main Avenue.

"Would you like treats for the dogs?" the young man at the window would ask. "Oh, yes, please," Mariam would reply, as knowledgeable snouts and tongues pressed forward to receive the creamy white dollops served in kid-size cups. Many other businesses, from the tollbooth at the airport parking lot, to the drive-up windows at the bank, stock jars of dog biscuits and dispense them to the local canine citizens.

Dogs are welcome most everywhere in Durango—certainly strolling the streets, provided owners obey leash laws, and browsing in stores. Shop dogs, like the amiable yellow Lab in Duranglers fly-fishing store, wag in welcome, or snooze with their heads sprawled over the thresholds. Outdoor patios at ice cream shops and coffee bars offer plenty of sunny naps for dogs, while their people chat with friends or peruse the paper.

It seems that having a large dog is a requirement for contractors and construction workers. Our small, lean, wiry landscape maintenance man has a huge chocolate Lab named Roger, who may well outweigh him. While all colors of Labrador retrievers seem to be favored for ride-alongs, other well-muscled and suitably happy mixed breeds also share the scene. A very well-behaved, gray-muzzled golden retriever was seen recently in repose just to one side of a massive cement laying operation, obviously the mascot of a worker, and also well trained not to leave paw prints in his owner's work.

Downtown street fairs bring out people and their dogs for a social stroll. Amid booths that display jewelry, hand-thrown ceramics, and fine carved furniture, you can find water bowls for dogs, special treats, and hand-sewn kerchiefs.

During our first full-time year, Walter designed and supervised construction of a music listening room, where he can retreat to listen to his vast, eclectic collection of vinyl recordings and CDs. Passionate and educated about music, he listens with intense concentration and immersion. The dogs join him, and seem to find deep relaxation when part of this experience. They also have the same reaction when I'm in there doing yoga.

For twenty-five years, Durango has hosted a summer festival called Music in the Mountains. During three weeks in July and August, some of the best classical musicians from the U.S. and overseas converge to present a rich and varied series of concerts under a huge white tent, nestled at the base of the Durango Mountain Resort ski area, about thirty minutes north of town. Each morning, the orchestra or chamber ensemble rehearses in the tent. People may attend rehearsals free of charge, to observe the behind-the-scenes skills of musicians and conductors, while they prepare for the evening's showcase.

Summer concerts, and indeed all events, are often challenged by the weather. Thunderstorms, sometimes fierce and raucous, can interrupt, ruin or revamp plans on a moment's notice. Rehearsals are no exception.

One warm summer morning, Walter and I arrived at the big tent with Sophie and Tucker. We planned to sit outside on the grass and enjoy the music. Soon, the skies threatened and the storm rumbled into action. Chased inside by the rain, the four of us took refuge in the back of the tent, uncertain if any rules restricted dogs from concerts. Hail began to pound so hard that it drowned out crescendos of music. Shrugging his shoulders and smiling, the conductor indicated a short break was in order. We unpacked our picnic on a utility table in the back of the tent and enjoyed lunch until the music could resume. No one ever said a word about the dogs, and they spent the time meeting and greeting other people and dozing under the table.

For the first two years, we reveled in the shift of the seasons, the diversity of skills, talents and life experiences of the people we met, and how well we fit into this new life. Scarcely a day went by that one of us didn't comment on our good fortune to live here, the joys the dogs found in their experiences, and our gratitude for whatever guided us to this place. We treasured our home, the land and the animals on it. But soon, these treasures were at risk, and we'd find ourselves powerless to save them.

Fire!

We'd just taken a red-eye flight home from Anchorage. After two weeks in the Alaskan wilderness and little rest on the return flights, I needed a nap. Sophie and Tucker gave us a great effusive greeting, although spending two weeks with our friend and house sitter, Linda, had been a treat for them. She let them lie beside her, while she did yoga, gave them Reiki treatments, and lavished them with love and attention.

I arose after several hours' sleep and groped into the bathroom, groggy and disoriented. I don't often nap, and usually feel worse afterwards. I glanced out the window to the north and snapped to attention. A huge, billowing plume of thick, black smoke chugged skyward, right behind our mountain.

"Walter—there's a fire!" I yelled and pulled on my clothes. He and the dogs joined me on the back deck to assess how close it was.

"I haven't heard any sirens yet," Walter said. "Let's drive up the road to see exactly where it is."

"Okay, but let's bring the dogs with us, just in case we can't get back home for some reason."

We joined a small procession of other curious residents also worried by the sight, and drove about four miles north, where the fire burned fiercely up Missionary Ridge Road that leads into the backcountry. We parked off the road and watched the first fire crews arrive to attack the blaze. Conditions were dangerously ripe for fire. Humidity hovered in the single digits, and temperatures were unseasonably warm, even hot, for early June.

"It looks like it's burning toward the east, away from homes," Walter said. "I think we'll be fine. Let's get out of the way and get a good night's sleep tonight."

So began the Missionary Ridge Fire on June 9, 2002. Each morning dawned with another layer of soot and ash that covered homes, neighborhoods and ranches that adjoined the burning acreage. *The Durango Herald* newspaper and local radio stations scrambled to provide up-to-the-minute reports. The number of firefighters grew daily, and a tent city mushroomed at the fairgrounds and local high school. The Red Cross, Salvation Army, churches and community organizations sprang into action to provide support services for the town's swelling population and those who were evacuated.

People deposited donated clothes and personal supplies in bins placed all over town. Announcements over the public address system at Walmart updated firefighter needs and directed shoppers to place their donations in bins at the front door. Within minutes, bags with shampoo, fresh socks and underwear, sunscreen, shoelaces and snacks filled the containers.

At the fairgrounds, volunteers re-supplied row after row of tables with fresh clothing and personal items that other volunteers delivered from the bins. Durango residents helped to serve three meals a day to hundreds of firefighters, took broken eyeglasses to be fixed, made face-shielding bandanas from donated fabric, sorted tons of supplies, food and bottled water, and set it all out for tired workers to pick up before they bedded down to rest.

Everything about this fire confounded the experts. It wasn't supposed to be this dry or burn this fast, or veer in the directions it did. It consumed dry brush lands and dense forests alike, and demolished centuries of thick growth with an offhanded, persistent carelessness. And it raged on for weeks.

It moved eastward, away from our property. Residents and visitors throughout town and the entire county gathered on street corners and alongside roads, stunned by the sight of massive, horrifying plumes of smoke. Our precious corner of Colorado was under siege, and it appeared that nothing could stop the monster's progress.

As it surged toward the tiny enclave at Vallecito Lake, residents were urged to park their boats, RVs and extra vehicles on the dry lakebed, where the drought-drained reservoir had shrunk to pitiful proportions. With only one mountain road for access, people were told to stand by for immediate evacuation.

But suddenly, the wild, lawless conflagration spun fire-generated tornadoes across the lakebed, sucking burning trees and RVs skyward in a horrifying display of nature's fury.

After it laid waste to parts of the mountain hamlet, the beast shifted and turned its attention back to the west, where the first sparks had ignited. Continuing to savage wilderness and homes in its path, the fire returned.

A sheriff's deputy hand-delivered the pre-evacuation warning to Walter and me several days later. We began to haul belongings in my horse trailer over to friends' homes far from danger. We piled boxes and bags in their guest rooms. We delivered our cat for safekeeping. She spent the next week huddled under a bed, bunking with several cats from other evacuees. She was safe, but unhappy. My horses remained at a friend's ranch, where we boarded them while we were in Alaska.

We stood our ground, until the afternoon an immense, choking cloud of black smoke oozed over our ridgeline and flowed toward us. The dogs already waited in the Yukon. Walter, so calm, hand watered our lush green lawn. With tears streaming down my cheeks, I fumbled in the garage for final items, and selected in my frantic state a handful of baseball caps to rescue. I posted instructions to fire crews on the front door: which doors were unlocked, where turn-off valves were, where our propane tanks were located, and a thank you for their efforts. We said a prayer and pulled out of the driveway, knowing the rules of evacuation: once gone, you couldn't return until given permission. Who knew when that would be?

Dear friends Steve and Victoria offered us their guest-house in Hesperus, a small community of sprawling ranches about twenty miles west of our place. We arrived for what the dogs must have considered a vacation. Now, they had forty new acres to explore, plus a free-flowing ditch of cool, fresh water. Making themselves right at home, they launched into vigorous exploration. Victoria's little dog, Shirley, was nearly overwhelmed by the big, lively goldens, but she politely avoided their attention and getting overrun.

Each day was the same: Turn on the radio for the morning fire update, eat, dress, run the dogs, and then load them up to drive back to the valley. We spent our days at Gail and Norm's house, with their two dogs. Sophie and Tucker seemed thrilled with this routine—new friends and a pond overflowing with water. From this vantage, directly across the valley from our place, we could track the fire's inexorable progress, as it crept and then surged southward, toward our home. Each evening, a different group of friends converged here to monitor the destruction. A potluck dinner always seemed to appear. We brought smoked salmon from Alaska. The gathering fed body and soul, and we comforted each other.

The next several days would become the crucible. I wrote of those days in an article for *The Durango Herald.*

In Praise
of Home and Heroes

Thursday night was hell. From a friend's house in The Ranch, we watched the boiling wrath of flames besiege the valley walls and flow like hot lava into the wooded grasslands. Trees torched, barns exploded, and the world before us burned with fury.

The blaze moved west, then south, toward our home.

I've lived where fire, floods and rockslides were part of life. I'm experienced with these disasters, but I guess you never get used to them. For days, weeks now, I've stopped to talk with any yellow-shirted fire fighter parked by the side of the road. They have been unfailingly polite and professional, and I've learned a tremendous amount about this fire. One day, a crew of three followed me home, and division chief Joe King walked our property with us. Joe is from Bozeman, Montana and teaches others how to fight fire. He felt we were pretty defensible, but offered a few suggestions: cut arching tree limbs, move firewood, rake leaves. We got right to it, and increased our odds.

Saturday was hell closer to home. After nearly two weeks of a vigil that had almost become a job, the moment of truth was at hand. After yet another dinner with our friends, we returned to "our spot" in the parking lot at Dalton Golf Course. From there, we could see our roof, our tall, stately ponderosa pines, Douglas firs and the cliffs behind.

This night, a growing, glowing, red cancerous fire, insidious in its expansion, lurked just above our property. We watched through binoculars, tracking every move. We talked to strangers, neighbors and the TV crew from Albuquerque. We never took our eyes off the cliff.

Rock and roll music from a party at the Dalton Club House mixed with the smoke and ash that swirled around us. It seemed at the least inconsiderate and at most intrusive. It was surreal.

My husband couldn't bear to watch. I couldn't bear to leave. If my house was going to burn, I wanted to see it. As a hospice volunteer, I saw importance in being there. If I couldn't save it, I could be witness to its passing. It was hospice for my house.

We compromised. We'd leave before our property was touched. But I'd return alone, whenever I awoke during the night.

I sat on a rock and talked quietly with my house. I said how much we loved living there. I said I was frightened, and knew it was, too. I said there were good people coming to help. I said goodbye.

Sunday morning, I arose at 5:00 and slipped out of the guesthouse in Hesperus. By 6:00, I turned onto Trimble Lane. A moment later, I saw our roof and our trees. I saw smoke rising all around, but saw neighbors' roofs, too. I cried.

I spoke with the checkpoint team at the barricade, but they offered little. I turned back toward Dalton, to sit and watch. Two fire command vehicles sat alongside the road, with two weary looking men leaning against them. I stopped there.

"Did you two have anything to do with saving my house?" I asked.

"Yes, ma'am," one replied quietly.

"Thank you so much," I said, and buried my face in his smoky, soot-stained yellow shirt. We held each other tightly, as my tears flowed.

Terry McShane from Carbondale had arrived just a few days before, to assume command for the night crews working along 250. Tony Harwig from Animas Fire supervised structural protection. While Terry lit the backfire some fifty yards above my house, Tony and his crew foamed the house and protected the barn and shed. It worked.

Terry filled me in on as many details as I could think to ask and he had energy to share. It had obviously been a long and stressful night. I kept saying thank you and asked him to tell everyone on the crew. "Would you like to thank them yourself?" he asked.

He radioed to the teams coming off the mountain to stop at the checkpoint. Half a dozen pickup trucks, a bus and a van paused with their passengers on the way toward food and rest. "You saved my home!" I exalted at each open window. Through their fatigue, they beamed.

I pulled open the door on the van, to find about twenty brawny young men stuffed inside, their faces obscured by dirt and soot. Only their eyes were visible. "You saved my house!" I said. "Which one was yours?" one asked. I described our property, and a couple of faces came alive. "That was MY house!" one said with pride. I thanked him profusely.

After they rolled on toward town, Terry had one more question for me. "Do you want to see your house?" he asked. I nodded and began to cry again.

First, he drove me up the road several miles, past dark sections of total destruction, and past homes still standing from Thursday's onslaught. From the road, the Bar D Chuckwagon appeared to be destroyed, but he said only the awning was singed. Then, we returned to my driveway.

All the buildings and tall trees appeared to be untouched—absolutely untouched. Some oaks and junipers had been cut down, and the wood stacked in tidy piles under the oak grove in front. Limbs had been trimmed, and left in the open. The hay bales in the barn had been strewn in the paddock. Fire hoses were still strung across the decks.

Above the barn and round pen, the firebreak had been cut. Bulldozers had mowed down a wide swath of oak and shrubs. Our fence lines were down, to allow the dozers through. From this point, they lit a burnoff that had consumed scrub oak on the top half of our property, to meet the wildfire that had burned above.

After a quick look around, and a couple of photos, we left. At the checkpoint, I met the man and woman who were crew chiefs. They, too, seemed satisfied. They had saved all five homes. It was a good night.

My husband and I were allowed to return several days later, for a brief visit. The grass was still green. My roses were in bloom. Several signs I'd scrawled hastily for the firefighters still hung by the front door, including my thank you note. At the bottom of it, someone had written, "It was our privilege and honor. (Signed) Pierre SD FD, John, Terry, Joe and (another name)."

Across the page, a different hand had written "Ditto. Rapid City SD FD." I was reminded never to underestimate the importance of place, or the kindness of strangers.

Yesterday, I ran into Terry McShane at the fire command headquarters. We hugged again, like old friends who had been apart too long. Last night, we also got to visit with Jay Adams from Oregon, one of the crew chiefs. We heaped more praise on his broad shoulders, but he turned the tables on us. "In eleven years, I've never seen such a warm reception from a town as we received in Durango. I'm not good with emotions like this, and it makes me choke up," he admitted. I learned his wife is a quilter, and he'd taken some bandana fabric (provided by the La Plata Quilters Guild) for her to make a "fire quilt."

Joe, Terry, Tony and Jay are new friends. They represent 1,271 other men and women who are working on the ground and in the air for all of us in Durango. We're blessed by their capability, passion and commitment. I want to thank them again and again. And I want to tell them they saved our home on June 22, the third anniversary of our move to Durango.

June 27, 2002

But the fire gods weren't finished with us yet. Several days after we escaped tragedy, and crews diverted the blaze back onto itself, fate struck again. Late one sweltering afternoon, one of the federal wildfire management officers stood atop Missionary Ridge, strategizing for containment of the massive blaze. He glanced across the valley to see another fire just starting. His first instinct was to contact whoever was in charge of that fire, when he realized no one was. He was the only one who even knew of it, so he had to take charge. He radioed to headquarters: "I want every plane and helicopter from the Missionary Ridge fire over here right now. Drop everything else and move it! We've got another fire!"

Residents had five minutes to evacuate. All north and southbound access roads into Durango were shut down. Visitors stood watching the incredible scene, alongside anxious residents trying to return home from work. Burly pickups with horse trailers were denied access to rescue livestock. Cell phone connections no longer worked. Power was cut from a large area, as officials feared another uncontrollable surge of destruction. By nightfall, more thick smoke hung over the valley. More homes had been lost. Residents reeled in shock and disbelief.

The wildfire manager later told me that if he hadn't assumed that responsibility, although it hadn't been delegated to him, this new fire would have surged through several counties with devastating speed.

After nine days of evacuation, we were allowed to return home. The bitter smell of smoke pervaded our house, but every structure and tall conifer on the property had been saved. The twenty-foot-wide dozer line that saved us was mitigated for flood damage by a fire crew using downed trees and boulders placed to divert mud and water flows.

Within a week of containment, local, state and federal officials held an informational meeting at Fort Lewis College. Still experiencing hot, dry weather, we left all the windows open at home, while we attended. During the evening, a strong wind arose and swept over the land. We returned home to find every inch of every room covered with a layer of black ash. Surveying the unmade bed, strewn with black soot, I burst into tears. Although this was a minor, annoying inconvenience, it seemed as if this disaster would never end. In the next week, cool summer showers arrived and we sang and danced in the rain, like prairie homesteaders celebrating the end of a drought. But the rains brought with them the acrid, pungent odor of burned trees and singed soil. Floods followed, inundating homes and properties at the foot of canyon runoffs. Roads were closed, while plows tried to keep up with flash floods and deep rivers of debris. The first floor of a neighbor's brand new home was buried to the ceilings in rock and mud. Creeks forged new pathways down denuded hillsides. Heavy equipment rumbled up and down our road, from one flood site to the next.

Re-seeding miles of burned land followed. I happened to be sitting on the back deck with the dogs when a low flying, fixed-wing plane began to make gridded sweeps overhead. The larger seeds in the blend fell to earth like small hail, rat-a-tat-tatting on the deck first, followed by showers of smaller seeds that drifted down from the sky. Puzzled, the dogs looked up, and then followed the sounds, only to find seeds carpeting the deck, filling their water bowl. I reassured them that this was going to help re-vegetate the land and save us from harm.

The Missionary Ridge fire was probably caused by backfire from a vehicle driving up the dirt road on June 3. A hot wire on pasture fencing that was designed to burn off low grasses caused the Valley fire. The fires burned from June 9 to July 17 when crews achieved containment. Hot spots smoldered for weeks. The devastation totaled 70,662 acres, fifty-six homes, twenty-seven outbuildings, and one death. Damage was estimated at $48,935,000.

Our sturdy and resourceful little community came together in recovery no less spectacularly than it had during the fire itself.

We give thanks every day that our place in paradise was spared. We were among the most fortunate of residents.

Daisy

Daisy arrived in our lives as if she'd been dropped on the porch by a helicopter dousing a blazing fire. Suddenly, she was there, and we had no idea why. Just as suddenly, the plan would become clear to us, further down the road.

On a bitter, gray Friday in January, I stopped at the La Plata County Humane Society to renew licenses for Sophie and Tucker. I filled out the forms and handed them to the pretty, blonde lady at the front desk. After perusing the data, she uttered those fateful words:

"Oh, golden retrievers. Would you like another one?"

I laughed and said, "I always want another one."

"A little six-month-old female was turned in an hour ago," Pretty Blonde Lady said with a beguiling smile.

My heart stopped. It was as if God himself had stepped into the office and said, "Here's your next dog." How could I not at least take a look at her? It seemed too perfectly orchestrated to ignore.

"She's still in quarantine, so I can't bring her out for you," said this woman, who was about to change our lives so dramatically. "But you can look at her through the window."

With a bit of trepidation—*What was I thinking?*—I peered into the back holding area. The pup was young, energetic and cute as a bug. I stepped back, took a deep breath, and said, "Okay, let me fill out the papers for her. But I have to bring my husband in to meet her, too, and our other dogs as well."

Breathing a little rapidly, my hand shaking just a bit, I filled out more forms and drove home to ponder what this would mean. We'd had three dogs before and it was a little more work, but so much fun. Of course, one of those dogs had been Nikki. We considered her more human than dog, since she was never cause for concern, always well mannered and a superb traveler.

But our household was so settled. At nine, Tucker was solid as a rock, placid and a kind, loving soul. Sophie was seven, still in her prime, energetic but polite, and sweetness to the core. Days were predictable, life was tranquil, and we were a congenial, comfortable family.

I fixed a nice dinner, poured Walter a second glass of wine, and then broached the subject. "There's a young golden in the shelter. She's just six months old and has already had two homes. What would you think about looking at her?"

"Well, she needs a home," he said, "and we have one." I was stunned. Maybe between God's intervention and Walter's receptivity this was meant to be.

Sunday afternoon, we took Sophie and Tucker with us to the shelter to meet Daisy. Walter and I waited in the private meet 'n greet room, agreed that if we both liked her, it was a done deal. The door burst open and a leggy flurry of blonde dog burst in, pulling on the leash. "Take as long as you like," the shelter worker said, and closed the door behind her.

By that time, Daisy had charged up to both of us, spun around the room at least three times and continued to sniff the corners, as if she were tracking a prime rib.

"She's pretty cute," Walter said.

"How can you tell? She hasn't stopped long enough for me to see her face or even put a hand on her."

We managed to reel in the whirling dervish long enough to pat her, appreciate her big brown eyes, and then, she was off again. Her frenzied energy should have been a red flag to me, but I was already smitten and had decided to go for broke. "Let's take her for a walk with Sophie and Tucker."

In the parking lot, we leashed up our two and let them jump down to meet Daisy. All three circled around, sniffed various body parts, and then seemed comfortable with each other. We walked up and down a bit, and decided the trio could work.

"Let's do it!" we agreed, and returned with Daisy to the front desk to finalize the deal.

Daisy needed to be spayed before we could adopt her. That was scheduled for Monday morning, so we could return in the afternoon to pick her up. When we arrived, she was still well under the influence of the anesthetic, but was given the green light to head for home with us.

Mindful of the issues involved in introducing a new dog into the household, we used metal exercise pens to cordon off a quiet area for Daisy in the TV room. Groggy and unsteady on her feet, she stumbled into her pen and slumped into a heap on her fluffy new bed. Sophie and Tucker circled around, curious, but polite, as we'd expected. Within an hour, poor Daisy vomited up an ill-timed meal from earlier in the day, and looked pitiful. We cleaned her up, replaced her bedding, and walked her outside. Then, I curled up in the pen, her limp body sprawled next to me, her head in my lap. "Oh, you poor dear," I said and stroked her gently. "You'll feel better in the morning." After we patted her goodnight, the rest of her new family trundled upstairs for bed, hoping we'd all sleep well and the sun would rise on a happier camper.

I padded downstairs the next morning, and was greeted by a new dog. Daisy, alert and perky, stood atop those long legs, grinning, begging to get the day started with a bang.

"Oh, no you don't," I cautioned and clipped a leash to her collar. "You're supposed to stay quiet for the next week, so you can heal." Daisy ignored my caveat, put her front paws on the top of the pen, and continued to wiggle from end to end.

"Off!" I commanded and opened the gate to walk her outside.

I could scarcely believe what I saw. This couldn't be the same sorry dog I'd cuddled the night before. With no sign of post-operative pain, no apparent memory of her upset stomach, and every intention of dragging me across the yard in pursuit of any evidence of wildlife, Daisy hit her stride way faster than I did that morning, and she would for years to come.

This being Tuesday, I was packing for a long-planned trip on Wednesday to visit friends Margo and Jenny in the Seattle area.

"Are you sure you're okay managing the threesome?" I asked Walter.

"Oh, sure," he answered in his usual casual manner. "How hard can it be?"

"Just keep everyone separated until I get home. Then, you won't have any worries or surprises."

Wednesday evening, I phoned home from Washington. "How's everything going?"

"Pretty good," Walter said. "Except she ate her leather leash."

"The whole thing?"

"Pretty much."

"How did that happen?"

"I didn't want to leave her home unsupervised, so I brought her skiing with me," Walter said. "I left her in the Explorer, with her bed and water. I guess I forgot to hide her leash. I called the vet and he said it would just have to work its way through her. But you have a good time and don't worry about anything here."

Hmm. This may be more of a challenge than we expected. But Walter still sounded cheerful, and he was trying to do the right thing for the new kid on the block.

Thursday night, I called again. "How did it go today?" I said, somewhat hesitantly.

"Today she ate the seat belt." This time, Walter sounded a little less enchanted with the leggy blonde. "I had a meeting in town, so I brought her with me. I even went out to check on her a couple of times each hour. She was always sitting in the driver's seat, looking out at the world. But as soon as I left, she must have returned to her work. She severed that strap as cleanly as if she'd used a scalpel."

Uh oh. Things were going from bad to worse. From a small price tag to a big-ticket item, the girl seemed to be setting her sights higher. But at least her first indiscretion hadn't caused any GI problems.

Over the next several days, when I phoned in to check on the destruction derby, Walter gave shorter and less detailed reports. All four of them were surviving, and I would be home soon. But it was a rocky start to life in the Pfau house for Daisy.

For the next week or so, we continued to set up pens and move barriers around the house, so Sophie and Tucker could become comfortable with Daisy's presence, while we observed doctor's orders for her incision to heal. They both seemed somewhat interested, but showed no hostilities toward the newcomer. Daisy, meanwhile, was stockpiling her unspent energy and enthusiasm to explore her new digs. When we thought it safe, we opened the doors to the back of the property for all three to become better acquainted.

Tucker trotted up the hill to sniff fresh tracks from whatever night visitors had crossed his domain. Sophie raced over the same territory with her usual speed and grace. But Daisy put them both to shame when she attempted a new land speed record, all the while sniffing, spinning and stretching those long legs.

The threesome returned to the back deck on this unseasonably mild and sunny February afternoon. We watched their interactions and felt pretty confident that this was going to work.

Then, Tucker voiced a different opinion. Daisy had sailed toward him, almost sliding into him on the deck in her eagerness to get a game going. From somewhere in the depths of his being, Tucker summoned a growl that meant business, claimed his territory, and set limits for the youngster. As if to say, "Get out of my face—NOW!" the ferocity of his snarl shocked us. Startled, Daisy found her brakes, and skidded to one side to avoid a collision. Undaunted, she scampered off to play with Sophie.

Daisy decided to return to the deck one more time, and again rushed Tucker to see if he'd changed his mind. Nope— this rebuff sounded even fiercer, a "Don't even think about it!" with severe consequences threatened if she did. This time, Daisy stepped back, almost with respect. They never had words again, although she'd occasionally hurtle toward him, realize her mistake, then change course on a dime, and remember, "Oh, yeah. You don't do play. Okay."

It was a very clear lesson in dominance from the pack leader. We'd never seen it from Tucker before, but never before had he needed to use it. Nikki had been the elegant matriarch for most of his life, and Sophie had never been rude, to his way of thinking. But this out-of-control intruder was another story. Tucker had spoken what we now realized: This girl needed some serious discipline.

Inexperienced with such a wild child, I needed professional help. That's when we found Mary Babbitt. A recent graduate of our local Fort Lewis College with a degree in business, Mary had combined her lifelong love of dogs with her solid experience training and showing dogs since childhood. With a newly minted business plan under her arm, she opened *Bravo!*, a dog board-and-train facility in Durango.

A spacious room allowed for year-round obedience classes, and indoor pens served as rest areas for doggie day care clients as well as overnight accommodations for boarders. The outdoor fenced area included a child's wading pool for water lovers, and room for every dog to stretch legs in supervised playtime. We liked Mary's gentle but firm approach, her smiling, twinkling eyes that never missed a thing, and Daisy adored her at first meeting.

We started weekly obedience classes, but found even that was insufficient to curb this girl's uncontrollable urges.

After three sets of classes, and good attention to practice, we knew we needed more. Since we'd scheduled a two-week vacation in Yellowstone quite some time before Daisy whirled into our lives, leaving her under Mary's tutelage for those weeks seemed like the perfect solution. Or so we hoped. Sophie and Tucker might also enjoy a vacation from Daisy, safe at home with our house sitter.

When we returned, Mary gave us a two-page document titled "Send Home Instructions." Sort of a report card, with directions for more homework, it started like this:

"Overall Daisy needs solid structure and discipline in her life. She hasn't been allowed to make many of her own decisions in the past two weeks and that has really changed her demeanor. Now, she walks nicely on a leash, waits at doors, doesn't jump, and remains in good control. The bulk of this has been accomplished by expecting and demanding respect and certain behaviors from her—all the time."

Wow. How could I have raised, owned, trained, worked and lived with four goldens over the past twenty years and not known how to do this?

But Daisy was a livewire who knew what she wanted and ignored everything to get it. She pulled on leashes, jumped on people, barked, charged across the property, ignored recalls, ate anything (and everything) in the landscape, and essentially ran wild. I had to keep up with Mary's good work or risk living with a golden grenade. There was only one choice.

Obedience?

"I think you're ready to enter an obedience competition," Mary said one day, after Daisy and I finished one of our many private lessons.

I looked around to see whom Mary had addressed. She can't have meant me, and certainly not Daisy. Yes, we'd made steady progress, but after just six months of work, surely we weren't ready for the ring.

"Yes, you two!" she said with a smile. "I wouldn't suggest it if I didn't think you were capable. I want my students to succeed, not fail. And there's a nice show in Grand Junction that's just a four-hour drive away," she added, as if it were a done deal. "Now, we have to get you registered, and get Daisy her ILP."

What's an ILP? Despite having dogs my whole life, I'd never done more than basic obedience classes and a few casual sessions of agility in California. Training for the hospital dogs was very specific and included little that seemed to apply to the show ring.

Purebred dogs registered with the American Kennel

Club (AKC) are assigned a number used for all event registrations and to track points and award titles. Dogs that appear to be purebred, but don't have papers, can be assigned an ILP (indefinite listing privilege) and are eligible to enter AKC-sanctioned competitions and earn titles.

Titles? I thought. *Not in this lifetime, and probably not in the next.* But I'll humor Mary and go along with this hairbrained idea of taking Daisy to an obedience trial. She took the required photos of Daisy, and together we filled out the application.

"So what will be her registered name?" Mary asked. "You already call your property the Glad Dog Ranch. Maybe something using that?"

"Umm, okay. How about Gladdog's Dashing Daisy?" That's kind of cute. And she sure is dashing—most of the time.

"Fine," Mary agreed. "Just sign here and I'll send it in today. We'll hear pretty soon if she's accepted and then we can put her ILP number on the show registration."

And just like that, we entered the world of obedience showing. Sure enough, Daisy was approved for her ILP, and a few weeks later, Mary and I loaded up my Yukon with enough gear to last the dogs and us for a month in the wilderness. At least it seemed that way. Two crates in the back for Daisy and the rottweiler Mary was showing for a client, suitcases, ringside gear for us, food, bowls, beds—it was never-ending. Away we sailed to Grand Junction.

When we arrived, I was overwhelmed by the size of the show. Hundreds of dogs were competing in conformation and obedience. We trundled past ring after ring to the far end of the huge, grassy park to set up our shade canopy, chairs and dog gear. A small contingent of friends from

Durango was also there, and this would be our little encampment for the weekend.

We unloaded more stuff at the hotel and settled in for the night. Tomorrow would be a big day for Daisy and me. We were registered for novice obedience on Saturday and rally obedience on Sunday.

Traditional obedience work involves performing exercises as directed by the judge in the ring. Rally obedience was new on the horizon as a demonstration sport. Rally courses require the handler and dog to perform a series of exercises, described on oversized cards, numbered and placed into a course. For example, in addition to the usual sit, stay, down and stand positions, the dog might be asked to remain in place while the handler walks around the dog. Or the dog and handler may be asked to weave together through a row of orange cones. Or to make tight left or right turns together, or to back up three steps together. Both forms of obedience require teams to enter at the novice level and move up the ladder, as points and titles are earned. Under no delusions, I knew we had a very long way to go to achieve more than mere entrant status.

Saturday morning, we motored over to the park and watched the advanced obedience classes that preceded Daisy's debut in novice. When our time came, I entered the ring under the watchful eyes of a kindly, bald gentleman, wearing a coat and tie and a bemused expression.

"Are you ready?" he asked, as we stepped up to the plate.

"Yes," I lied to him, all the bystanders, other competitors and God himself.

"Forward," he commanded.

Off we surged. Daisy tugged on the leash, nose pinned to the ground. I corrected her, but still she snuffled in the grass.

"Right turn," the judge sang out, and Daisy and I careened to the right, the leash tight as ever.

"Left turn," he directed, and Daisy and I collided, as we lurched left. She looked like she'd never been on a leash, let alone trained.

"Halt." *Okay, we can do this part,* I think. But Daisy wouldn't sit, and her head bobbed from side to side, as she took in all the scenery around her.

This little parody continued as it had started—disjointed, distracted and disobedient, through the entire exercise. Nearing the end, the judge peered over his glasses at me, our score sheet on his clipboard riddled with demerits. "Would you like to *try* the sit stay?" he asked. His expression read, *"Or would you rather leave the ring now and not embarrass yourself any further?"*

"We might as well try." Sit she did, but sprang right back up. Same with the down stay. Finally, mercifully, it was over.

We left the ring, with Daisy still tugging and pulling toward my friends at ringside. Darla came forward, laughing.

"Well, Holli, at least she didn't bite the judge!" she said. We all hugged and laughed, and Mary joined in.

"There. You've had your first ring experience and you're still alive," she said. That was the best she could offer about this dubious performance.

"I think this isn't for us," I said. "Maybe we'll have a better run at rally tomorrow." Of course, I had no empirical evidence to support that hope.

The next morning, we weren't due at the field until around noon, so Mary and I loaded up the dogs and stopped to browse at Borders Books. The sky clouded over, but didn't yet threaten rain. I left the front windows open a bit and we headed for the store.

I rambled to the back to browse the stacks. In just a few minutes, Mary came looking for me. "I think you might want to put up the windows—it's raining hard now."

Sure enough, it was pouring, a real cloudburst. I slogged through ankle-deep water in the parking lot to put up windows, despite the small flood that already soaked the front seats. Dogs fine, people sopped.

We waited it out a bit, but realized this was going to be the weather *du jour* and knew we had to head for the show. While the conformation rings had posted rain delays, obedience continued. We huddled with our dogs and friends under one of the shade canopies, now dropped down to half height. It shed water in sheets. Hunched over in our chairs, we peered out to see when we were expected to brave the storm and strut our stuff.

Daisy is impervious to weather—rain, snow, wind, thunder, lightning—she takes it all in stride. I knew we had that going for us. Maybe little else, but at least that.

We approached the ring and entered on the judge's request. Entrants had been allowed to walk the course first without their dogs, so I prayed I could remember the order and exercises required. In rally, the handler is able to talk freely to the dog, use hand signals, and repeat commands as needed. You can use your entire body from the knees up to help direct your dog. I figured I'd need it all to keep Miss Busy Body in tow.

"Are you ready?" came the now familiar or infamous question.

"Yes," I once again fibbed, sounding more confident than I felt.

"Forward," came the command.

On leash for this novice course, Daisy started with me,

and stayed reasonably close by. "Good girl!" I praised. At least our first five steps were a success.

The course was easy, especially since this was a demonstration of the new sport, and we weren't out to earn points toward a title. *Like that would happen today.* We cruised from station to station, stopped, Daisy sat, she lay down, she heeled (sort of), and she even looked up at me. What was happening here? This is pretty cool, and we're not doing too badly.

And then, it was over. Daisy sprang up for a hug, tongue lolled to one side, wide smile on her face, and looked for Mary to garner even more praise.

"Pretty darned good, you guys!" we heard.

"Not bad at all," someone else offered.

"Better than yesterday," a pundit observed.

I was amazed—we'd done it! Through rain, wind and nerves, and insecurities and many missteps along the way— we'd done it. There might be a future for us after all.

Girls' Day Out

It was a lovely spring morning, with some overcast and showers forecast for the afternoon. All three dogs took advantage of time outside in the sunshine to peruse the property and gather evidence of all that had transpired under the recently melted snows of winter.

Tucker ambled with his nose to the ground for scents and information on ground squirrels, chipmunks and other local residents. During the morning, he returned to the back deck, now bathed in sun, and sprawled, paws tipped over the deck edge, nose lifted to the breeze, eyes half closed in sheer pleasure and appreciation of the good life. Now ten years old, Tuck knew how to pace himself.

The girls, meanwhile, took a far more active approach to the same pursuits. They sped uphill, then raced down, chased, spun, changed direction, and took off again. Good smells and the occasional small animal lured them, and they ran with abandon.

Sophie interrupted the chase for a big, sloppy drink at the dish on the deck. She flopped next to Tucker, grinned and panted. Tireless, Daisy maintained her patrol.

Suddenly, some sound, movement or disturbance had

their attention, and all three charged straight up the back of the property, past the barn and toward the rock-faced cliffs. I watched, smiled at their intensity, and appreciated the athleticism of the young girls. Soon, Daisy and Sophie scaled the lower flanks of the hill, as they sometimes did in pursuit of noisy rodents. They dodged back and forth, criss-crossed paths, and moved ever higher up the cliff.

By this time, Tucker had returned to the deck and gave me his "I'm no trouble to nobody" look. I reminded him that on occasion, he and Sophie had managed to escape outside our ten fenced acres, and we had to drag their sorry little behinds home from a neighbor's property.

When I turned my attention back to the girls, I was shocked to see that they'd somehow breached the safety of our fence and nearly reached the top of the cliff edge.

"Sophie! Daisy!" I yelled again and again, but to no avail. I could tell that the call of the wild had once again lured them toward some seductive reward. I alerted Walter, and he started up the hill to trudge the faint game trail that elk use to move from the valley to high altitude meadows for spring and summer.

But today, there were no migratory animals, just our two young goldens, charging off into the vast San Juan National Forest toward who knew what perils.

Walter tracked them for a while and caught glimpses, but never gained on their speedy charge. He returned to the house and we planned our search.

"Let's each take a car and head in a different direction," I suggested, while I pulled on a jacket and noticed clouds rolling in. "Grab your cell phone, so we can stay in touch."

Our road runs parallel to the valley, on the east side. Walter headed north, cruised slowly, called out, and watched for blonde heads to emerge from the oak brush alongside the road. Steep cliffs climb behind the sprawling properties and occasional homes. It was impossible to see where they might have gone. Once on the Missionary Ridge trail system, they could run for miles into untracked wilderness.

I turned south, still on our road, pulled into neighbors' driveways, called out, and remembered where we'd found Sophie and Tucker during previous forays. Nothing.

We reunited at home. "Not a sign," Walter said.

"I have no idea how to get up there," I said. There were trailheads north and south of us, but then which way to go?

Back out on the roads again, we ventured farther afield. I stopped at the golf course. "Have you seen a couple of blonde golden retrievers down here?" I asked a foursome in a golf cart.

"No, we haven't." I left my card and asked them to call if they did.

The afternoon wore on, skies blackened, wind came up, and rain began to spit on our efforts to find the wayward girls. We silently feared the worst. Accident, injury and attacks all crossed our minds. We had to press on.

While Walter stayed home to phone neighbors, I took off again, this time across the one-mile wide valley, out to the main highway that leads north to Silverton. I began to look up and down for bodies. As fast as these girls can run, they could have covered this distance and faced sixty-mile-per-hour traffic. Relieved when I found nothing, I returned home.

In the near dark with steady rain, our spirits flagged. It'd been six hours since we'd last seen the girls. Our efforts had been fruitless. We were almost out of daylight and options.

"Let's take one last slow drive up our road," I said. "It's

the direction they headed. We'll leave the front gate open, so they can run in." Tucker was safe and quiet in the house, and we patted his big head before we left one more time.

With heavy hearts under blackening skies, we pulled out and turned north. We stopped at several homes on the way, left our card, and pleaded for them to call. We were both wet from the rain, dirty from hiking hillsides and across properties, and must have looked distraught as well. Several miles north, we turned around and crawled toward home. Our hearts and bodies ached and we slumped in our seats. By now, people were returning from town and work, so there was a little more traffic on the road. That scared me, as I inched along, headlights on high beam to catch any glimpse of blondes.

"There isn't anything else we can do tonight," Walter said, his voice low. "We'll just have to leave the gate open and all the lights on for them."

"We've never lost a dog," I said, holding back tears. "I don't want to start now."

We drove on in silence. Rain fell and night descended.

Suddenly, something moved on our side of the road. I slowed and peered into the gloom.

"What's that?" I asked, almost not daring to hope. "It's them!" I yelled and pulled the car over, so Walter could jump out.

There, trotting single file, were two of the dirtiest, filthiest, wettest, and maybe happiest golden retrievers I'd ever seen. Daisy led the duo, moving at a good clip. Sophie followed right behind, her beautiful, thick tail and pantaloon fur chock full of burrs, branches, weeds and sticks. They both turned when we called, tongues lolling out and muzzles covered in mud, but great, wide smiles spread across their faces.

I couldn't tell if they were glad to see us or were expressing joy at their grand adventure.

"Get in here," we commanded, opening the back of the Explorer. Both girls leaped inside, panted, shook off water and mud, and pushed up front to snuggle.

"Get back!" I yelped and ducked to avoid the slime on a long, dirty tongue.

They must have traveled miles cross country to collect so much debris in their coats. The mud probably came from a good romp in the irrigation ditch behind properties across the street. Maybe they even made it to the river a little farther west.

We drove south, through our gate, to the safety of home. In the cold rain, we pulled the flotsam and jetsam from their fur, bathed both dogs, towel dried their shivering bodies, and settled in the warm kitchen to give thanks and gather the whole family together, safe and sound.

Tucker sniffed them each, rallied around our group, and looked up as if to remind us once again: "I'm the good boy. I'm no trouble to nobody."

Turkey Day and Other Wild Encounters

During the seven years we lived in Arcadia, California, we enjoyed viewing wildlife from the vantage of our deck, cantilevered over the Wilderness Park preserve. Sheltered by ancient, arching cottonwoods alongside the creek, deer meandered on the trails. Families of quail scurried through the underbrush. Owls hooted to each other through inky nights, and sometimes perched above the deck to swivel their heads and watch the dogs in wide-eyed wonderment. Then, silently, they soared over the canyon in search of sustenance.

Early one morning, I heard grunting sounds just outside the sliding glass door of the bedroom. Since only the screen was closed, I arose to peer into the dawn light. Startled to see a black bear shambling on the deck around the pool, I pulled the glass door shut before the dogs could burst through the screen to protect their territory. The big beast must have been drawn to the water and decided it was worth the effort to mount the cinderblock walls or wrought iron fencing.

Bears frequented the neighborhoods near us, and one nicknamed Sampson had been photographed on more than one occasion, enjoying a soak in a family's hot tub. Mountain lions were also reported, and residents were urged to protect their children and pets when the big cats were on the prowl.

We'd become accustomed to wildlife, even before we moved to Durango. But life on nearly ten acres that adjoin a national forest and then the vast Weminuche Wilderness, one of the largest such tracts in the U.S., put us on even more intimate terms with wild animals.

Tucker, for some reason, took immediate exception to magpies. These big birds, over twenty inches in length and with a swagger that would be the envy of any gunslinger, taunted the dogs. Chase as they would, the dogs never nailed one of these aggressive and brazen birds. I recently wished they could, when I witnessed a magpie pin a grosbeak to the ground and peck at its breast. I flew downstairs and out the front door, bellowing, "Don't you dare do that!" which caused the magpie to pause just long enough for his victim to escape.

On a summer day, as Sophie and Tucker trundled across the back property, I realized a chase was about to begin, more intense than the occasional excursion after a jackrabbit. I looked up in time to see the dogs in pursuit of a lean young coyote. The very startled animal was stretched out in front, with Sophie the Swift next in line, and Tucker the Slower bringing up the rear. They crossed the entire property right up to the south fence line, where the youngster didn't see the four-by-four inch woven wire fencing. He rebounded backwards from it as if he'd bounced off a trampoline. At the same time, Sophie and Tucker also recoiled, startled at this turn of events.

The coyote spun on a dime, regained his equilibrium, and

flashed back across the land. The two dogs circled around and downshifted. I knew Sophie was just enjoying the chase, and that Tucker hadn't a prayer of catching up, so I marveled at the young coyote's speed and extension when he found his overdrive. He led the dogs back to the south fence one more time and cleared it, leaving my pack of two panting at the edge of what might have been.

I try to be very aware when deer cross the property, as they often do in spring and fall, to graze the upper reaches in back of the house and barn. Daisy announces deer sightings with a very specific bark and warble. Because I don't want the dogs to practice behavior that is illegal, I let them set up a ruckus at the French doors or stand on the guest room bed for a better view of the hillside and the passing parade. Sorry girls. No chase for you.

Bears frequent the neighborhood more in autumn, to gorge on ten thousand calories a day to prepare for winter hibernation. If early spring freezes damage the native berry or acorn crops, then hungry bears move toward human habitation and food sources, such as trashcans, pet food, fruit trees and bird feeders. Starting in August, the ursines travel many miles a day in search of food. At the first sign of these visitors, we bring trashcans into the garage and reduce the number of bird feeders to a couple that I can bring in after dark.

One October night, Walter took Sophie and Tucker out for their evening constitutional. There had been no signs or sounds of critters, so the three of them strolled out the garage door and toward the upper grass in front. Suddenly, Tucker let out a startled "Woof!" and found reverse gear the same time a black bear bolted in the opposite direction. It was a toss-up who was more startled.

Some mornings, there is ample evidence, often with undigested apples from our trees, that we've been visited overnight. When that happens, the dogs go on high alert. They scan the property and race the fence lines to be certain intruders have left the premises.

Perhaps the most elusive sightings here have been bobcats in the spring. Early one morning, I spied a pair of the wide-footed felines cruise down the back hill toward the house, supported on a crust of freshly frozen snow. The tufts of hair that curled from their ear tips made me think they could be lynx that were reintroduced in the area. But no, they were bobcats. My view was cut short when the dogs spotted the cats and barked a warning that sent them back up the hill.

Daisy gets the most bang for her buck from the rodent families that emerge in spring to taunt, entertain and frustrate her well into autumn. From the first tiny chipmunk that sets her throat warbling to the last ground squirrel to vanish, she makes the most of it. On point at the window or French door, she doesn't move a muscle, her eyes sink deeper into their sockets, and her breathing all but stops. Once let loose on the run, she flies like a heat-seeking rocket after the unsuspecting creature that hightails it for cover in the nearest rock, hole or drain pipe. Daisy then sets up camp next to it, and sometimes stands for a half hour before she settles down to lie in wait for the next move in this chess game. I only wish I could elicit the same focus and attention for obedience or agility.

Abert's squirrels raise the bar even higher. These graceful, full-tailed creatures sport huge ears relative to their size, which give them a startled expression. They spend more time in trees, but do come to earth to forage and pick up nuts and seeds. As fast as the dogs are, they'll never beat an Abert's to a tree, so they're left to stand with front paws on the trunk and peer upward, while the squirrel rummages in the branches overhead.

Wild turkeys roam in spring, in pairs or trios, often higher on our hill. But one morning, a whole armada of the chunky, graceless creatures had settled in the front yard, just feet from our picture window. Still half asleep, I shuffled toward the front door, to let the dogs out for their morning pit stop. For some reason, I glanced at the bird feeders in the front oaks and saw a whole flock of turkeys, chowing down on spilled seed. I turned to shepherd the girls out the back door instead. Once relieved, they hustled in for breakfast, while I marched out front to flap my pink bathrobe and urge the turkeys to vacate their feeding station. They turned, blinked in disbelief, and continued to dine, unperturbed by my intrusion. "Shoo!" I ordered and flapped. They blinked some more. One or two took a few slow steps aside. I trudged into their space with more authority, and they grudgingly began to leave the treasure trove of good eats. I urged a few across the driveway and into a neighbor's yard. Others broke away from the group and strolled toward the oak grove. I came back in the house where the dogs licked their bowls after breakfast and still had no clue what was up outside. Good. Hysteria averted.

About an hour later, I checked both front and back yards. No sign of turkeys anywhere. The coast was clear. I opened the back French doors, to let the girls slip outside for their morning explorations. Without a moment's hesitation, they charged across the flower garden, behind the shed and up the dirt road to the barn. Suddenly, dogs and turkeys exploded everywhere, the birds flushed from their repose behind the barn and out of my sight. The rodeo was on.

As if on cue, the dogs split the flock in half, each to pursue the lumbering, flapping, startled birds. But instead of flying into the trees, the dumb-as-a-post turkeys ran only far enough to escape each dog's charge, and then turned to stare in disbelief when the charge kept coming.

The dogs spun wildly, almost flustered by this embarrassment of riches. Which to chase next? A few birds lifted ponderously into the air and perched on branches in the tall pines above the reach of the dogs. Others lurched over fences.

One tough old bird remained ground bound, still trying to outrun the frenzied dogs. Daisy was closest and turned her sights on this prey. Fast as lightning, she stretched out full length and covered yards in only a few well-propelled strides. Just when I thought I should heat the oven and prepare stuffing, she leaped a good four feet off the ground, jaws agape and ready to make contact. The bird mustered one final, desperate flap to become airborne, and escaped by mere inches Daisy's grip and certain fate.

Glad I didn't have to clean up a bloody aftermath, I returned to the house and left the girls to cool down with lots of sweeps across the land, just in case a bird remained. I was almost sorry that Daisy's energetic effort hadn't fulfilled her genetic legacy as a bird dog.

The Best Doc in Town

One of the first things we did when we arrived in Durango was ask about veterinarians. With three dogs living on ten acres and hiking miles of wilderness trails, we wanted to be prepared for unforeseen emergencies and maintain good preventive health care in our new environment. Even before we moved here full time, we knew we needed to be ready.

On recommendation from Mariam, our friend with six dogs, who had also worked at the humane society, we met Dr. Larry Cohen of Baker's Bridge Veterinary Clinic, just six miles north on our road. A genial, solid man with strong hands, soft voice and a gentle nature, Larry had also moved to Durango to retire, after years in practice in southern California. But after a brief time of boredom, he spotted the Baker's Bridge practice for sale and succumbed once again to his passion. The property included the small clinic right on the banks of the Animas River, as well as a handsome log home. The clinic's crackerjack vet tech Jill lived in the home on the other side. It was meant to be and Larry was back in the game.

PURE GOLD

That first summer, our initial meetings were over simple things. Tucker split a nail on a front foot and it wouldn't stop bleeding.

"Is he good?" Larry asked me, as he contemplated a quick procedure versus anesthesia to accomplish the same thing.

"What?"

"Is he a good dog?" Larry said, while he continued to assess Tucker's temperament and held the bloody paw aloft.

"Well, yes," I said, not sure why this mattered.

"Okay then," Larry gave the nail a fast clip into the quick, and then cauterized it. Tucker's immediate wail of pain subsided. Larry offered a biscuit in apology for the sudden action, which Tucker accepted with his usual polite manners.

"Yes, he's a good dog," Larry said, patting the big head, while he reinforced the new relationship with more biscuits. "I couldn't see putting him under if he could handle that, and he did just fine. Good boy," he said again. Not one to hold a grudge, Tucker accepted more biscuits.

After that first summer I spent in Durango, I returned to L.A., where I'd left my horse in the capable care of his trainer. Early that autumn, I was trail riding with friends when our small group encountered several riders my trainer hadn't seen in some time. While they visited, one rider in the group began small talk with me. When she asked where I lived, I said Durango—well, not totally, and first I had to sell our house here, and actually, I'd just spent the summer there.

"Durango? Well, if you ever need a good vet there, I can recommend one to you. When I lived in Woodland Hills, he saved one of my puppies from parvovirus. Then, he did surgery on my older dog. He's just the best diagnostician I've ever known. I was so disappointed when he moved to Durango."

144

"What's his name?" I wondered who this marvel was and how far away his practice was from our new home.

"Larry Cohen," she answered. "You must get to know him."

"I already do." What a small world, and how lucky I was to have found him. Little did I know how important that relationship would be.

During our first several years in Durango, it seemed like the dogs were always ingesting some luscious—to them—morsel. On hikes in the mountains, it could be remnants of someone else's picnic lunch, or maybe a chicken bone or two. It might be scat from any number of small animals, or something even grander.

One day, we climbed up the flanks of nearly thirteen-thousand foot Engineer Mountain where Tucker found a prize: an elk femur. Big, thick and redolent with essence of the wild, this bone was worth fighting for. He suddenly turned possessive, a trait we seldom saw in this gentle giant. He paraded it in front of Sophie, and then growled when she came to investigate. We chastised this behavior and flung his treasure over a cliff edge, while we hung onto his collar to prevent a launch after it. There would be others, we assured him, but he'd have to share.

Back at home, the dogs never tired of thorough searches behind the house, up the hill, for enticing discoveries. I forever yelled, "Get out of there," especially at Tucker, when he slunk under the paddock fence to grab a mouthful of that wonderful stuff horses produce in prodigious quantities. I mucked out the stalls and paddock daily before breakfast, but when I let the dogs outside, the stuff was just too tantalizing. The manure pile was also a lure, but not nearly as much as the fresh stuff. Larry assured me this coprophagia was normal, natural and not nearly as harmful to canines as it was disgusting to humans. But the dogs were still banished when they arrived at the back door with green lips and tattletale breath.

One day, Tucker became terribly sick, heaving until there was little left to heave. It was so sudden, intense and body wracking that we rushed him up to Larry's.

"Sure looks like he ate something pretty bad," Larry's associate vet Rick Bayer said. Tucker continued to wretch and roll his eyes. "Let me keep him today and tonight, to get some IV fluids going and try to calm his stomach."

We left the poor lad and waited for a report later in the day. He wasn't much improved, so we began to troll the property to see what he could have eaten. After a thorough search, all we could conclude was maybe he'd nibbled one of those nasty looking black mushrooms that had sprouted on the manure pile. We phoned the information to Rick and he thumbed through toxicology texts to do further research.

Day by day, Tucker hung on. Walter and I visited him at the clinic, and were shocked to see his weight drop each time. His eyes looked sunken and the skin sagged on his beautiful head. Rick was in touch daily, and often several times, with Larry who was on vacation. They collaborated on treatment plans and worked to keep Tucker alive. "I'm just not ready to let him go yet," I murmured softly one afternoon after a visit. "He's only nine years old, and such a dear boy." We went home to pray some more.

That night, Jill, their more than dedicated vet tech, stayed with Tucker until 3:00 AM. The next morning, we got a call.

"I think he's turned the corner," Rick said, sounding optimistic. "You can take him home tomorrow. We just want to make sure he can keep some food down now."

We arrived to bring home our now painfully thin boy. He wobbled out to greet us, and we all hugged and shed a tear of joy together. "This was touch and go, you know," Rick admitted. "But we're sure glad he pulled through. He's a sweetheart, and such a good patient."

We thanked them profusely, grateful to pay the bill and bring Tuck home to put on some weight and spend more years by our sides. The next day, I delivered two fragrant home baked apple pies to the clinic. "There's no way I can thank you enough," I said, and gave hugs all around again. "But maybe you will enjoy these." I also gave Jill some chamomile tea, so she could get a good night's sleep.

Not every visit to the clinic was so traumatic. While Nikki and Tucker remained cautious about their stops there, Sophie viewed every single occasion as a social call. She trotted in with confidence, greeted staff, other patients and their people as her personal friends, and held court. Full of joy, sporting the happiest tail in town, and twinkling those eyes mischievously, Sophie could brighten the darkest day. Big dogs, tiny pups, yowling cats—she took them all in stride and tried to spread her sunny outlook everywhere.

One afternoon, when I arrived to pick her up after a dental cleaning, the receptionist laughed. "That little Sophie," she said. "What a flirt."

"How so?"

"Even before she was fully awake from the anesthetic, she wagged her tail," the woman replied. "Whenever one of us walked by her cage, she'd wag and then cast those flirty little eyes our way. She's such a cutie."

Sure enough, Sophie emerged from the back with every bit of sparkle that she'd displayed in the morning. Even with eyes still hazy from the drug, she stopped to take in everyone else in the room, and then weaved her way to the door.

Daisy, on the other hand, doesn't know which way to go. Although cautious of the medical environment, Daisy thinks Jill is one of the best people on earth, so she is thrilled to see her. She also has another very special friend, who joined the staff the first year that Daisy was thrashing our household and upending our lives with her energy and disregard for authority.

I arrived with Daisy for some minor checkup. When I walked in, I noticed a new person at the front desk.

"Hello!" she said brightly. "May I help you? I bet this is Daisy." She looked down on the desk to pull out her chart.

At the sound of her voice, Daisy sprang onto her hind legs to see who was behind the counter. Pretty Blonde Lady stood up to meet Daisy's long nose coming toward her.

It was her! The lady from the humane society who had fatefully said, "Golden retrievers—would you like another one?" It was her!

Pat and Daisy had a whirlwind reunion. Pat came into the waiting area and Daisy all but knocked her down with enthusiasm. We chuckled over this turn of events, and I "blamed" Pat for all the challenges we now had in our lives. To this day, Pat and Daisy share a special bond of rescuer and rescued. I always see it in their eyes. And Pat knows she was right on the money when she spotted me for Daisy's forever home.

The chicken dinner is another on Walter's list of memorable episodes, while caring for the dogs when I was out of town.

This time, I'd hauled my horse over Wolf Creek Pass and La Veta Pass—yes, going anywhere in Colorado involves scaling at least one mountain pass—to a friend's ranch in Stonewall. After several glorious days of trail riding, I arrived home at dusk, happy and tired from the wonderful experience. I pulled the trailer up the hill to the barn and Walter trudged up to meet me, his expression dark.

Without so much as a "Hi, welcome home. How are you?" he said, "Daisy ate a chicken."

Not sure if she'd stalked this prize herself and enjoyed a raw meal, or been rude at the dinner table, I asked what happened. I off loaded my horse and pitched some hay into the paddock for him.

"I brought home a rotisserie chicken for dinner," Walter said. "After I ate my portion, I left the rest on a plate at the back of the kitchen counter, for you. In a little while, I noticed Daisy wasn't with Sophie, Tucker and me in the TV room. When I got up to look for her, she was in the living room."

"What makes you think she got the chicken?"

"Well, it wasn't on the plate anymore. And all I found in the living room next to Daisy was the little plastic ring they put around the legs to hold them together."

"That's all?"

"There wasn't a speck of chicken anywhere. Not on the floor or the rug or anywhere. She ate the whole damned thing—except for the plastic leg holder."

Walter knew how dangerous cooked poultry bones can be to a dog's intestines, so he'd called Larry. There was little he could advise, except to keep an eye on her and hope for the best.

Daisy must have ground those bones up in her strong jaws, because she suffered no ill effects. We realized how lucky we were and pledged not to let this happen ever again. But to this day, when we bring home a rotisserie chicken, her eyes light up, and her hopeful expression says, "Oooh, chicken. My favorite!"

Two at the Bridge

The August morning dawned bright and clear, a day that could grace any Colorado calendar. Up early to take Tucker to the vet, I relished the drive north through our summer green valley, with the Twilight Peaks a dramatic backdrop.

Now eleven, and slowed by age, Tucker had developed a few cysts and assorted small lumps on his skin. When he scratched them, they bled, and it was a challenge to get them to heal. With a clean pre-op blood panel from the week before, he was scheduled for minor surgery to remove the most offending growths.

After an uneventful procedure and a quiet day with his friends at Baker's Bridge, Tuck was discharged late in the afternoon. Despite the early morning anesthetic, he seemed quite hung over when I picked him up.

"Sometimes, it takes a little longer to clear the anesthetic from their systems," Larry and his staff reassured me. "And he's getting older, so just give it some time. Remember—only a little water at a time and no dinner until he's back to normal."

Once home, Tuck chose to sleep off his binge, and Sophie stayed close by. The evening wore on, but his condition didn't change.

Then, Sophie began to pant, and sought refuge behind the toilet in the guest bathroom downstairs. She seemed uncomfortable and unable to settle. I phoned Larry after dinner. I was concerned about bloat, although she hadn't had any exercise after her evening meal.

"It sounds like it could be indigestion," he offered. "Try walking her outside to see if that relieves her discomfort. Call me back."

Now, we had two troubled dogs. Tucker wobbled outside with us, and Sophie tried valiantly to walk up and down the driveway. She soon collapsed and lay outside on the front pathway. She still smiled up at us and wagged her tail, but something was obviously wrong.

"Larry, she's not even on her feet anymore."

"Bring her right up," he said, despite it being 10:00 PM.

I left Tucker to sleep undisturbed, and Walter and I raced back up the valley. Larry had the clinic open and switched on the front porch lights when we arrived. We carried Sophie inside, and Larry's expression suddenly turned serious.

"Oh, my God," he said softly. "I think she's dying."

His big hands expertly took her vital signs, and checked her gums and abdomen. He aspirated fluid from her lungs, and she lay gasping for breath.

"I'm afraid it's her heart," he said. "I'll do what I can to stabilize her tonight, and I'll call Jill over to be with her. But I'm afraid it's not going to be good news." Stunned, Walter and I got in the car and returned home, hugged the still impaired Tucker, and slept fitfully until dawn. At 7:00 AM, Larry called.

"I've confirmed our worst fears. Her heart is tremendously enlarged, so it now fills 75 percent of her chest cavity. There isn't room for her lungs to function, and they're filling with fluid. I've spoken with the cardiac specialists in Santa Fe and there really isn't anything we can do for her."

I hung up the phone and told Walter the news. We held each other in shock and tried to think. We didn't have to discuss the options because there weren't any. We couldn't let her suffer.

I made arrangements for her euthanasia later that day. I felt once again submerged in that suffocating fog of disbelief and pending doom. She was only nine, and hadn't shown any symptoms. Sure, she'd slowed down a bit from the downhill racer of her youth, but that was to be expected. Her sparkling spirit remained as bright as ever, yet soon she'd be gone.

Tucker was barely improved in the morning, but we clung to every tiny ray of light on this now very dark day. He ate a bit and drank some, but when he eliminated, I was disturbed at the dark color of his urine.

The tears flowed all day, our hearts breaking, and our bodies in physical pain at the prospect of losing our little sprite. Of all our dogs, Sophie was the brightest star, the sweetest soul, and the kindest friend. We'd expected she'd carry her engaging personality well into old age.

"Let's take Tucker with us, to say goodbye to Sophie," I said, when the time came near to drive north once again. Walter nodded, as heartbroken as I.

We arrived at the end of the clinic's scheduled patients and were greeted by staff members with very long faces. "She's still trying to flirt with us," said Jill. "Her tail wags a little bit whenever I walk by."

Larry's wife, Kristi, was also there to comfort us. "I'm so sorry to hear about Sophie," she said and draped an arm over my shoulders. "She's such a great dog."

But before we saw Sophie, I wanted Larry to check Tucker, who still hadn't recovered from yesterday's anesthesia. His gums looked pale, the whites of his eyes jaundiced, and he was obviously struggling. Larry checked the boy's vital signs. "He just hasn't bounced back," he said. "After his illness two years ago, his liver and kidneys may never have functioned normally." We nodded dumbly, and lifted Tuck down off the exam table.

Ever mindful of details at such times, Jill had spread a beautiful white quilt on the grass of the riverbank behind the clinic. "You go on outside," she said softly, "and I'll bring Sophie to you."

We led the still wobbly Tucker outside and sat down on the quilt. The sky had never been so beautiful. That clear Colorado blue with clouds as light as my heart was heavy. The river gurgled with summer runoff. Sophie loved to swim. This was her kind of day.

Jill arrived with our girl and laid her gently beside Tucker. With her remaining strength, Sophie smiled, wagged weakly, and leaned against Tuck.

Walter and I sat, quietly murmuring our love to each of them, stroked their heads and bodies, and tried to put that memory forever in our hearts. Sophie's smooth, blonde coat was as thick and fluffy as ever. Tuck's auburn coat had seemed to dull and turn brittle overnight.

I paused, searching the skies for guidance. "Walter," I almost whispered, after a while. "Should Tuck go with Sophie today?"

"I was thinking the same thing," he said quietly, reclining alongside his boy and also looking deeply into the summer sky.

I let that thought hang in the air between us, to see where it would settle. This decision had to be for them, not for us. There was nothing more we could do to heal them. It would be our final gift. And it seemed right that they should depart as they'd lived, side by side.

I walked back into the clinic and told Larry of our decision. He looked startled, but said nothing to dissuade us.

A short time later, he and his staff and Kristi gathered around us on the quilt. He and Jill took Sophie's paw and expertly led her to the edge of this realm. "Goodbye, dear heart," I whispered, my hands holding her beautiful little silver fox head. "Go find Nik and Bo."

A moment later, Tucker whimpered when the needle entered his skin. "Go in peace, big boy," I guided him, and kissed his broad head. "Nik and Bo are waiting for you."

Then, they were still, on this exquisitely beautiful day, on the quilt on the grass, by the eternal river.

When we were finally able to stand and breathe, we returned inside the clinic. After a big hug, Larry looked me in the eye and said, "You made the right decision. I didn't want to say anything, but just know it was the right thing to do." He wiped a tear away and we thanked all of them for their kindness.

On the drive home, I said, "That was the most beautiful way to send them onward." Walter nodded, staring vacantly out at the valley, but unable to speak.

When we arrived home, Daisy tried to get our attention, but we began to sink deeper into a pool of shock and pain.

Suddenly, it became clear why she'd been delivered into our household. Without her, it would have been unbearably quiet. We gave thanks for her energy that tried to fill the emptiness. But we knew this grief would linger, just as our memories of this unfathomable day would be with us for a long, long time.

The next morning, I could still hear them all around me. Tucker's big, gentle feet padding across the floor. His soft breath next to me by the fireplace and his woof at the door.

I heard Sophie's song, pure, sweet and clear, in perfect harmony with the world.

And I'll always hear them at dawn and dusk, in the cascading notes of the canyon wren.

Transitions

It happened at the gas station in town. Three days after losing Sophie and Tucker, I was pumping gas into my Subaru. Tears streamed down my cheeks, my mind in a fog, and my heart shrouded from the world, leaking pain into my body, like an inflamed wound that couldn't heal.

I was sleepwalking through my days, and trying to find solace at night from the overwhelming grief and emptiness that enveloped both of us.

Why haven't I heard from them? I wailed inside. I always hear from my dogs when they leave us. Nik and Bo had sent such affirming messages. Why haven't I heard from Sophie and Tucker?

Suddenly, like the flash of light during a mountain storm, they were both there. Sophie arrived first, dashing in from her new dimension, just as she used to fly at breakneck speed down the hill behind the house. Tucker followed shortly, and both were breathless.

"We're sorry—we never meant to upset you," Sophie began to apologize. "But we've been so busy. We're looking for your next dog," she chirped.

I stopped dead in my tracks, hand poised on the gas nozzle still in my tank. Not wanting to break this spell and desperate to hear more, I didn't move a muscle.

"Yes," Tucker joined in. "It's gonna be a boy. Yup, a nice, big boy," he proclaimed.

"No, no, no," Sophie interrupted. "It's a girl. It's a girl! It's a girl!" She cheered and danced around Tucker.

"Are you sure?" Tucker asked, no longer positive about his position in the face of Sophie's assured declaration.

"Yes, it's a girl! She's coming soon. We gotta run now, but please don't worry. We're fine and it's a girl! It's a girl!" She twirled with excitement, and Tucker shrugged as if to say, "Well, okay by me. But are you sure?"

Then, they were gone. Just like that. They were gone.

I pulled the nozzle from my car and replaced it in the receptacle. I snapped the tank cover shut, and walked behind my car to the driver's side door. I got in, turned the key, started the engine, released the brake, and slowly pulled away from the pumps and onto the street, heading north and home.

What had just happened? It had taken my breath away, and I could scarcely think. But I was comforted to the core to have heard from my two beloved and departed spirits. They were fine—that was the most important thing. They were fine.

They were already looking for our next dog. How wonderful! The power of that brief moment began to seep into my mind and my body. I could almost breathe again without aching in every cell. Everything that had been so tight and tense began to soften. "Thank you."

Tucker, the dominant member of the pack, had put Daisy in her place. She ranked number three beneath sprightly little Sophie. Now, low-on-the-totem-pole Daisy had lost not only her entire pack, but also her sense of place and order. She was elevated to alpha by death and default. It was a lot to take in, especially for a youngster not noted for her wisdom or perception. Smart she was, but sensitive, not always.

Perplexed over the sudden change in her household, she seemed to seesaw between ecstasy at being the only one to receive all our attention and the uncertainty of the tremendous change. One day, we sat side by side on the floor, and she turned to look deeply into my eyes. "Since they're both gone, will I be leaving next?" she asked me. I wrapped my arms around her, and promised that she wasn't going anywhere. I realized that in our sudden and massive grief, I'd never sat down and explained to her exactly what had happened. So, just as you would with a child, I held her and told her the whole story. She absorbed my words and emotions and seemed more settled. She sighed, got up slowly, shook from tip to tail, and appeared ready to move forward. For the first time, I saw Daisy move thoughtfully toward the future.

Within weeks of losing Sophie and Tucker, I started to open those familiar doors in the rescue world, knowing our next golden was already out there, somewhere, waiting for us. Despite the constant ache in my heart and the physical fatigue that accompanies grief, I already longed to welcome a new golden heart to help heal mine.

Larry composed this letter of recommendation to accompany my inquiries to rescue organizations:

> *"To whom it may concern:*
> *I am writing this letter to recommend Holli Pfau for whatever she wants to do when it comes to the welfare and safety of animals. I have known Holli for a decade and can certify her as being the best thing that could ever happen to a dog in need of an excellent and caring home. Any dog she may adopt, buy, happen by, or otherwise acquire would be like that animal hitting the power ball lottery."*

Because we now lived distant from any metro center and golden rescue program, I had to cast a wider net this time. I contacted groups in Arizona, Utah, New Mexico and Colorado. All had dogs that needed homes, but some restricted adoptions out of their state. I focused on Colorado and connected with Golden Retriever Rescue of the Rockies, or GRRR. I'd met Mary, their capable president, at the big dog show in Denver the prior year, and was impressed with their display and dedicated volunteers.

We journeyed to Golden for a golden. What better place, we agreed, to bring a young, cheerful breath of fresh air into our lives? Still mourning our recent, painful double losses, Walter and I brought Daisy along to pass judgment on prospective family members. We met Mary at a small kennel where GRRR houses goldens-in-waiting. One by one, she paraded the candidates before us.

Charlie was the first suitor. Eager, almost assaultive with enthusiasm, Charlie twirled around my legs, wrapped the blue leash tightly, and still he pulled. A flurry of freshly washed, long and silky bronze fur, he burst out the door and lunged down the quiet street toward the manicured park. Charlie hardly noticed I was there, indifferent to the human on the leash in his bolt for the greenbelt. After a brief tug-of-war, I returned him to the kennel's front desk. Bring me Bachelor number two.

Mary unloaded Midas from her dog-equipment-strewn van. "He's such a snuggler, and so sweet," she said because she'd shared her bed with this immense, lanky dog the last few nights. Sweet he was, but huge, and getting larger before my eyes, he unfurled himself and found his footing atop long, tall legs. He moved with the gentle, shambling gait of an Irish wolfhound. In fact, he looked like a wolfhound. And his history was fraught with skin, allergy and other medical problems. Maybe Bachelor number three?

Copper-coated Tobias tumbled from the van and peered with the red-rimmed eyes of a dog recovering from anesthetic. "He was neutered today, and I just picked him up from the vet," Mary explained. Even in his drug-induced stupor, Tobias noticed that Daisy was a perky blonde, and he proceeded to press his formerly manly self on her and elicited a well-deserved rebuke. Maybe a Bachelorette next?

We met Hunter, shy and setter colored. She seemed unable to connect with any of us. Big, robust Lacey burst through the gate, anarchy on a leash, and we demurred. Solid, blonde Tucker seemed a reasonable soul, but had a history of dogfights. Not in our calm household, we said. Boisterous Bailey regaled us with choruses of howling warbles, as he writhed on the ground in an uncontrolled frenzy.

Golden retrievers all, but they were as different and distinct as their life histories and personal baggage. We knew the right family would come along for each of them. We thanked Mary and departed with our only child. It isn't every day you get to pick a friend for life. Maybe tomorrow.

We headed home deflated. How could we have met so many dogs and not found the right one? "We'll know it when it happens," Walter reminded me. "We just didn't fall in love this time." I stared out the window and settled back for the long drive. I knew he was right, and had to believe that our next dog was out there somewhere, and I'd just have to keep prospecting.

I called Margo in Washington the next day. Margo and her lively red golden, Tangible, had been part of PAT in Pasadena before she moved north. She'd been active in golden rescue in L.A. and had fostered and owned many lovely dogs. She remained connected to breeders and friends in the golden network. Maybe she'd know where to turn next.

Very much a take-charge person, Margo set a search in motion. She called and e-mailed her contacts and kept me posted on the progress. At first, it was slow. No one seemed to have a young dog for us. Then, one day our fortunes changed.

"Holli, I've received only one lead on a dog for you," Margo said when she called. "And surprisingly, it's in Colorado, too. Jeanne von Barby, a well-known and respected breeder in Evergreen, has had a dog returned to her and is looking to place her. She says the dog is high energy, but don't be put off by that."

I reminded Margo that I had one of that flavor and I wasn't looking for any more energy, attitude or issues. I had a girl who already took way more time and energy than all four of my preceding goldens put together. And that was saying a lot.

"I think you should call Jeanne and talk with her," Margo urged. "You have nothing to lose and maybe she'll know of someone else with a dog."

I trusted Margo and knew she was right. But I was still hesitant.

Chatter

I met Jeanne in stages. First, there were e-mails: Yes, she had a young dog that needed a home. How had I been referred to her? What did I know about golden retrievers? Would her dog get plenty of attention and be a working dog? She wanted details to qualify me as a potential good owner.

Then, there was the telephone interview. Jeanne was polite, but cut to the chase to get the information she wanted. She sounded businesslike and buttoned up and was dedicated to finding the very best home for her dog.

Jeanne did say her youngster was high energy and needed some training, but vouched for the ability she'd seen in her so far. "But I do need to tell you one thing," she cautioned me. "She does have a cowlick down her nose."

That took my breath away. Sophie had also had this on her nose. Her first vet called it her racing stripe. In the conformation ring, it's considered a flaw, but for me, it was a wonderful sign. Sophie had indeed found this girl for me, right down to her signature stripe.

With no other prospects in sight, I prayed that this young dog would be the one. But there were certainly issues.

Although she had good genes from one of Jeanne's bitches and a well-known stud dog in New Hampshire, Chatter hadn't had the best start in her little life. While her siblings were all in good homes and learning how to be happy, healthy, working dogs, Chatter had struggled.

For the first time in more than twenty years of breeding, Jeanne had taken the word of a friend who vouched for Chatter's first owner. Yes, it'd be a fine home. That turned out to be wrong.

The woman worked and was gone for ten to twelve hours a day. When she arrived home, she was confronted with a lonely puppy. She complained that the dog was hysterical and she didn't know what to do. To her credit, she did take Chatter to early obedience classes and she did well. But this needy youngster had missed the loving, nurturing attention she needed to thrive.

Once Jeanne learned about the situation, she took immediate action. The dog would be returned to her for another placement. Unfortunately, she was traveling, so several friends took in little Chatter until she could once again be part of Jeanne's pack and gain some of what she lacked.

Jeanne wanted just the right home for this now nine-month-old pup. If Daisy liked her, if I thought I could train her, if she wasn't too over-the-top in energy, if the stars aligned—we'd have our next golden.

We decided to meet halfway between our homes, and Jeanne and I set a date for mid-September in Salida, a small mountain town tucked at the head of the broad San Luis Valley, alongside the Arkansas River. I drove up the day before and enjoyed the autumn beauty of the snow-dusted Sangre de Cristo range that framed the wheat-colored pastures piled with last cutting bales of hay. Ever the enthusiastic traveler,

Daisy roamed the back of the Yukon, watched the scenery stream by, and didn't miss a thing on the journey toward her next buddy.

We overnighted in a small, simple motel that welcomes dogs, complete with biscuits at the front desk and a freshly laundered dog bed in our spartan room. I pondered the challenges that lay ahead, stroked Daisy's golden head, and hoped this girl would be a good match for Daisy's high energy and strong opinions.

We walked through town the next morning, energized by the crisp, brisk day. I kept an eye on my watch, and drove to our designated meeting spot. We waited excitedly for Jeanne to arrive. Right on schedule, Jeanne and her friend, Linda, pulled up alongside us.

"Good morning! How nice to meet you. How was your drive? Pretty autumn, isn't it?" Jeanne pulled out a leash and prepared Chatter for her introduction.

A beautiful, sleek, medium golden dog smiled almost shyly at me, and I reached forward to greet her. "Oh, Jeanne — she's gorgeous!"

"Yes, she is," Jeanne said. "Let's get her out and introduce her to Daisy."

The two blondes sniffed casually at each other and seemed ready for a walk, so off we went along the river. "Chatter absolutely loves water and is quite the swimmer," Jeanne explained, when her dog pulled toward the riverbank. "She has a beautiful water entry." Jeanne has bred, shown and trained her dogs for fieldwork for years. She doesn't want her dogs to be just pretty faces; they also have to exhibit the talent and excel at the work for which the breed is known.

Petite and trim, Jeanne brightened the gray morning in

a red polar fleece jacket atop crisp jeans. Her close-cropped salt-and-pepper gray hair reminded me of Audrey Hepburn's early cuts. High cheekbones and attentive eyes supported the comparison. Simple gold jewelry polished the look.

She handled her young pup with poise and skill, gained in years of handling dogs—guiding, re-directing, encouraging and praising. Over lunch, she explained the lineage and titles of parents and siblings. "Her registered name is Elysian's Bundle of Rumours, and I liked Chatter for her call name," Jeanne said. "And she has a very good recall, too." *What a plus,* I thought, *compared to Daisy's erratic responses.*

I shared my story and Jeanne and Linda listened compassionately. While the dogs waited in our cars, it became obvious that Chatter would be allowed to join our pack of one. I wrote a check to Jeanne and we prepared to head for our respective homes.

We walked the girls one more time before we hit the road. Daisy loaded up without hesitation in the back of the Yukon. I didn't know how Chatter had been trained to ride in cars, so I'd brought a wire crate with a thick fleece pad for her. Jeanne and Linda hugged her goodbye, and she jumped up into the crate, turned to face me, and lay down. In her dark brown eyes, I saw a look of such uncertainty and discomfort, of resignation and insecurity. I'm sure after the many impermanent stops along her journey, she assumed this was just the next one.

"Let me know how she's doing," Jeanne said.

"Do you want daily reports?" She nodded and stroked Chatter's head one last time.

I settled into the driver's seat, turned the key, and then swiveled around to check on both girls. The radio piped up, a familiar song from the 60s: "This time the girl is gonna stay, for more than just a day." If only Chatter could know how true that was. By late afternoon, the autumn sun skimmed the higher peaks and vacated the valley. A blustery rain shower hopped and skipped through the pastures. A vivid double rainbow seemed to pace our speed south. *That's a good sign.* I smiled. *A very good sign.*

Dusk deepened and we climbed above the valley into Wolf Creek Pass, at 10,850 feet, one of the steeper and higher passes that connects western Colorado to the rest of the state. A busy snowstorm enveloped us, and I shifted to four-wheel drive and lowered my speed. I carried precious cargo and wanted to arrive safely in Durango.

The miles rolled by, while the girls slept. Chatter had no way of knowing she was on her way home, to her forever home.

Walter came out to greet us under the glare of the garage entry lights.

"Isn't she beautiful?" I beamed and opened the back of the Yukon to let the girls jump down into the yard.

"Well, it's a little hard to tell," he said. The two dogs stretched their legs and relieved themselves on the lawn. "But I'm happy that you're happy," and he led us into the house.

Over the next two days, the girls seemed comfortable with each other, and Chatter explored the acreage and the house. Smaller than Daisy, and not as leggy or lean, she carried a little more weight and the immature look of a dog in full adolescence. She'd come into season just a week before, so we outfitted her with panties, to keep any discharge from spotting our carpets and floors. This seemed quite the oddity to her, and to Daisy, too. But they ran and chased and played and burned youthful energy.

Late in the afternoon on the second day, they started a game of chase in the front yard—down the driveway, across the lawn, bounding up the boulder terrace and into the oak grove, then back again. They picked up speed, egged each other on, and began a rough and tumble tussle on the grass.

Watching this escalate, and hearing playful grunts edge into a few low growls, I decided to intervene.

"There, there, now, girls," I said with authority. "Let's keep this playful. What do you have to argue about?" They stepped back and eyed each other with suspicion.

They shook off the energy and ambled across the yard, friends once again. Later, when I called Jeanne to give her a progress report, I described the episode. She laughed. "My dear, that's why they're called bitches. Once Chatter is finished with her hormonal surge, things will settle down."

Daisy must have been asserting her position as top dog and Chatter thought about challenging it. Daisy persisted and now their roles were established.

We began to see that although they were the same breed and about the same color, these two girls were as different as two goldens could be. Tall, speedy, reactive and dominant, Daisy seemed to take all in stride, and approached every element of life with bravado and confidence. She knew what she wanted and went after it—a squirrel, a walk, attention or dinner.

Chatter, on the other hand, hadn't received the confidence gene and had spent her first nine months as a gypsy without roots. The combination left her with some deficits. When meeting and greeting, her submissiveness caused her to urinate, sometimes profusely. She groveled for attention, turning her belly skyward. She cringed and hesitated when we asked her to jump into the car and often relieved herself, sometimes on people's feet. Once coaxed or lifted into the car, she beat a hasty retreat to cower against the front seats. No amount of cajoling or treating made any difference.

What a needy girl she was. Jumping up—boisterously or gently—she pinned herself against us and all but cried for attention. This could escalate into a frenzy, and she jumped up to see us eye-to-eye and howled and barked. If we didn't meet her needs, she escalated to bumping our faces and even grabbing and pulling my hair with her teeth.

Once again, we called Mary to our rescue. She agreed with our assessment and suggested a number of solutions and techniques to divert, change and manage the behaviors. Some days these methods worked, some days they didn't. Daisy and Chatter fed off their youthful energy and inattention, and brought out the worst in each other.

In a matter of weeks, our calm, orderly household with Sophie and Tucker had devolved into days of flying feet and fur, frenzy and frustration. Daisy and Chatter ran wild and we wrung our hands and wracked our brains.

Walter was stalwart and supportive. "I know we can get through this. It will just take time and effort."

"Yes, I know. But having these two little firecrackers at the same time is almost more than I can handle." Success with four goldens before these two raging whippersnappers had done little to prepare me for this bewildering task.

I just have to keep my focus and not get discouraged. Then, Chatter began to spring skyward and pull my hair. "No!" I growled at her. There would be no rest for the weary.

Chatter
Channels
Sophie

The next months, I seesawed between frustration and joy, between tough love and tenderness. So, at first I didn't notice the similarities. I was too focused on managing all the frenetic activity in the household.

The two girls seemed combustible, like meteors that barely avoided collision, all day long, every day. They seemed to play "Can you top this?" with wild chases up and down the hill, races after anything that moved outside, and boisterous competition for Walter's and my attention indoors.

Their adolescent energy streaked off the charts. Although eighteen months older, Daisy lacked the maturity to guide Chatter toward a mellower take on life. Instead, Chatter's issues and insecurity only weakened Daisy's tenuous grasp on self-control, and all hell broke loose.

Walter and I couldn't let up for a minute or our positions as pack leaders would be overthrown by the two anarchists who threatened to rule the roost. I saw few glimmers of hope on the horizon, and exhaustion set in.

Then, Chatter would slip her head into my lap and roll her eyes upward to meet mine. Or nose my elbow for attention. Or parade through the living room with a section of Walter's Wall Street Journal in her mouth.

Still, I didn't make the connection.

Then, our shoes began to disappear. We couldn't find a matched set of slippers, because Chatter had carried one of each out into the yard and deposited them smack in the middle of a fresh snowfall or way out under the grove of oaks in front. Even Walter's heavy boots weren't safe, since the little lass could wrestle one of those at least out onto the driveway from the garage. Small as she was, she could drag a boot.

But the Chatter-Daisy tornado continued and the dust they kicked up clouded my vision.

"Chatter! Come back here, honey. Bring it to me." I often heard Walter cajole Chatter to return with some morsel she'd nosed out of his office wastebasket. It became a morning ritual for them, and was a sweet reminder of how Sophie had done the same thing.

With the speed of a receding glacier, the frenzy began to subside, from ninety miles an hour to just eighty. I still stepped aside to let them hurtle down the stairs, and bent my knees to lessen the blow when they rounded the corner from the living room into the kitchen. But we did notice the household was just a tad quieter.

I began to see more and more of Chatter's sweetness emerge once the pace of life slowed a bit. She never left my side in the house. She calmed with any touch of our hands. When hysteria vacated, she sought to fill the space with love and affection. And there was that dear cowlick stripe down her nose. Her gentle, loving ways began to surface.

Despite her wild habits outdoors, Daisy had always been reliable inside and had earned full house privileges when we weren't home. Chatter seemed likely to follow in her big sister's footsteps, so we gave them the run of both upstairs and downstairs when we left. But Chatter let us down, big time.

We returned from town one afternoon and looked in horror at the living room area rug. A two-foot length of one edge had been stripped bare and a hole the size of a dinner plate gaped alongside. Walter and I were almost speechless at the destruction. Daisy's expression told the whole story: "I didn't do it, Mom, I swear. I told her not to, but she did it anyway. Oh, this is very, very bad."

We cleaned up the mess and assessed our options. This was a brand new and expensive Persian rug, so we planned how to salvage the situation. "I think we can turn it around," Walter suggested, "and hide the mess under the back of the sofa." We hefted furniture and wrestled with the big rug to position the offense out of sight. "See? That works out fine." Walter, the perennial optimist, can always find sunshine in the darkness.

We hoped that episode was a bizarre aberration. A few days later, we were proven wrong.

"She did it again! That little dog did it again!" We gazed at the wounded rug to see another injury, inflicted on the fresh side. A small rug nearby had also been attacked. "That's it. No more house privileges for either of you." I felt sorry that Daisy had to suffer along with Jaws, but from then on, they'd be confined to the guest bedrooms when we left.

Over dinner that night, Walter reminded me of other rug incidents. "Don't you remember that Sophie used to nibble on the fringe and corners of the rug at the front door?

She'd pull off just a few bits of it and nothing else would be touched."

He was right. Bill Stavers had said he thought it happened within the first ten minutes after we left and was Sophie's method of stress management. She nipped off just a bit, probably stood up, shook herself, and said, "There. I feel better now," and lay down to sleep.

Unlike Bodie, who could have played outfield with any major league baseball team, Chatter lacked the skill to pluck a ball from the air. Although she loves to chase any thrown object—ball, toy or stick—she waits until it's ground bound to retrieve it. Sophie did the same thing.

I finally began to recognize the similarities in Chatter's and Sophie's phobias. Each was plagued by fears, triggered by specific actions. These energetic girls could be paralyzed in the face of some stimulus that certainly predated their arrival in our household. Through some grace of God, they each had been led to our safe haven.

Winter melted off into spring and summer, and the river calmed to a glassy green flow just down the road from our house. To burn more of Chatter's energy, we added a new dimension to our walks: The Swim. On warm mornings, we turned off the road along the river at the unofficial boat put-in and headed straight for the swimming hole. Chatter couldn't contain her excitement and once let off leash, sped to the river's edge to launch into the flow with her wonderful water entry. She pushed off from shore, floated through the air with her legs tucked aerodynamically under her, before she splashed in, and turned to see where we'd tossed a stick or ball. Daisy joined in, but seemed content with just a few dog paddles to cool off. Chatter, on the other hand, could swim forever and had to be coaxed or tricked to resume our walk.

She sought water wherever we found it—small creeks, ponds, lakes or irrigation ditches. They were all the same to her. Even a bit of mud suited her, like someone else we'd known and loved.

The constellation of coincidences couldn't be denied: the sweetness and the spunk, the needs and wants, and the presence in our lives. Sophie really had sent Chatter to fill a huge empty space.

Agility

"She has so much drive," Lynne said. We watched Daisy careen across the agility course and dive into the irrigation ditch water with amazing speed and total disregard for us.

"Is that what you call it?" I sighed. I sighed a lot these days. It seemed our agility career would be over before it could begin. "This is supposed to be a team sport, and I'll never be able to keep up with her."

"Oh, that's where training comes in," Lynne assured me. "You can do it. I know you can."

With that bit of encouragement from a very experienced trainer and successful competitor, we embarked on our journey into the sport of dog agility.

What would be a good outlet for Daisy's endless energy and might also channel her high-strung personality into productive activity? I turned to agility. In California, I'd taken Tucker and Sophie to a few classes. Tucker was happy to run two or three rounds on a course, albeit slower each time, until he settled ringside, a happy grin on his face that said, "There. That's enough for today." Athletic and speedy, Sophie loved to race through three or four obstacles, then dash to the sidelines, unable to control her wiggles. "Did you see THAT?! Now watch THIS!" and she was off again. I don't remember ever being able to run a full course with her, despite her obvious abilities. She was just too distracted by her love of people and the lure they provided at the field. So, agility was just a fun Saturday morning outing with my happy dogs and nothing more.

Daisy, on the other hand, needed a job. Something that would use her sharp mind and physical prowess. Something that would get her to focus. Something that would wear her out. Something that wouldn't kill me.

We started with Lynne's Obedience for Agility class. Despite Daisy's hard won success with Mary, applying those skills out on a wide-open field chock full of smells and water in the ditch eluded her. But we persevered.

Our first Introduction to Agility class was only a bit more successful. Daisy loved to fly over the jumps, dash through tunnels, and race up the A-frame. Trotting over the dog walk and mastering the teeter would take more time, but at least now we had something to work with.

Others in our class ranged from the elegant little Shirley, a petite mixed breed, affectionately known in our area as a rez dog (a stray picked up on one of the Native American reservations), to Zeke the Streak, who was cut from much the same cloth as Daisy. A young and exuberant standard Schnauzer, Zeke and Daisy played one-upsmanship to see who could fly around the field the longest, totally out of control and ignoring their handlers' entreaties to "Come!" Sometimes, this display lasted well into class, while others moved on with their education. Zeke's owner Gay and I chased, begged, coaxed and pleaded with our dogs. One

trainer required me to bring Daisy to class wearing a har-
ness, so we could fish her out of the ditch when she charged
into the water.

Shirley learned every obstacle, never ran off, and performed just as her owner Victoria requested in her neat
New Zealand accent. I told Victoria that Shirley always did
the course as if she were drying freshly applied polish on
her toenails. Perfect and precise, but without passion. They
abandoned their agility endeavors early on.

Gay and I joined the Durango Agility Dogs club (DAD),
to support their activities and purchases of equipment. We
were even a little embarrassed, thinking other members
would shun obvious incompetents, such as we felt we were,
but we figured our money was a good as anyone else's.
When no one sent our dues back with a letter declining
our memberships, we sighed in relief. Still, we felt like out-
casts, or at least poor relations. We tried to practice when
no one else was at the field to see our pitiful attempts at
training.

"Are you going to the agility club Christmas party at
Ginger's?" Gay called to ask.

"Nah. I don't really know anyone except you."

"So, how are you going to get acquainted then?" I
couldn't disagree, so we went, husbands in tow. They even
let us in the door—it was either our good fortune, the kindness fostered by the season, or that no one recognized us
as the bumbling dolts who struggled with Zeke and Daisy.

All of us settled around Ginger's comfortable living
room and enjoyed a delicious potluck dinner. Then, club
president Lynne posed a question. "Let's go around the

room, and I want each of you to share what your goal is for agility this next year."

Experienced competitors spoke of their hopes for titles, speed records, amassing points for their MACHs or NATCHs—still Greek to me. I squirmed in my chair when all eyes turned toward me for my proclamation. "I hope that maybe Daisy and I can do three obstacles in a row." Everyone laughed. But I was serious, and felt so intimidated by all these successful people with well-trained dogs. I just knew none of them had ever faced a challenge like Daisy. The lyrics from a song in *The Sound of Music* seemed appropriate: "How do you solve a problem like Maria?" Substitute Daisy and you get the picture.

After our first summer, I gained an immense appreciation for what my club mates could achieve. The following February, Gay and I and our friend Gail wanted to see the real thing in action. We went to the big Colorado Kennel Club Show in Denver at the huge complex where the National Stock Show is held.

In the main building, pandemonium was barely contained. Dogs of every breed recognized by AKC competed in conformation in ring after ring. Tall, elegant, silky-coated Borzois waited ringside with their handlers. Energetic, tightly wound border collies followed handler instructions with intense concentration. More mellow retrievers of all kinds strolled on loose leashes, smiling and greeting strangers. Big dogs, small dogs, novice entrants and champions mingled in palpable anticipation.

Upstairs, a tense hush lay over the obedience and rally obedience rings. Handlers whispered commands and rehearsed and practiced with their dogs outside the rings where judges presided over tests of skill. Seasoned exhibitors, seeking ultimate titles, looked as nervous as those attempting their first novice runs. Pewter dishes, clocks and china and ceramic bowls awaited the winners, displayed on tables alongside the coveted ribbons.

Throughout the venue, vendors sold every food, treat, toy and kind of merchandise for dogs you could imagine. It was like seeing all the pages of pet supply catalogs come to life: wire crates, cloth crates, cages; beds long, wide, narrow, deep, fluffy and sturdy; grooming combs, brushes, sprays, shampoos and conditioners; rawhide chews, pigs' ears, squeaky rabbits, squeaky balls and squeaky everything. Shoppers endured the crush, often with dogs by their sides, to fulfill every want and need of dogdom.

Booths for breed rescue organizations displayed before and after photos of painfully thin, sad-eyed dogs alongside their now healthy, beaming faces. Volunteers paraded dogs, hoping for new and compassionate homes. Sales of tee-shirts and calendars helped support their efforts.

Noontime fly ball demonstrations added to the cacophony. Handlers could barely contain the over-the-top obsession of border collies racing side by side.

In a totally separate building, the huge indoor riding arena, two rings of agility provided inspiration and intimidation for us novice wannabes. We observed from the tiered seating above the arena, amazed and astonished at the level of partnership exhibited by some teams, including several from our own little club in Durango. We watched, slack-jawed, as expert-level teams (mostly with border collies) flew through the courses flawlessly.

"Can you believe that?" We gasped, time after time.

"Amazing, just amazing." None of us dared even consider working at that level, or performing in this hallowed space.

One handler stood in the middle of the arena and silently pointed out the course to her dog that we later learned was deaf. Another handler, missing one leg and moving on crutches, guided her border collie to perfect scores. How humbling! I remarked to Gay, "So what exactly is *our* problem?"

"It has to be us," she said. "Our dogs could be wonderful."

She spoke the truth. In any sport or activity, the best make it look easy. But success comes from long, hard hours, and weeks and years of practice. We'd have to keep trying.

Daisy and I stumbled onward. She obviously loved what she was doing at the field, although it seldom resembled the tightly maneuvered courses our classmates managed to navigate. Then, one day, there was Daisy, doing three obstacles in a row—my dream come true! But it was only mid-year, so I might as well raise the ante and go for broke—how about a whole course of twelve or fifteen obstacles? What the heck? At least we provided entertainment for our classmates and our long-suffering, patient instructors.

Little by little, we could see the light go on for Daisy. "Stick with mom, follow her gangly, graceless cues, and then I get some treats. Cool." Week after week, class after class, practice after practice, we persevered. Most of the time, we had fun. Well, Daisy always had fun. High-spirited and talented, she had enough enthusiasm for both of us. But I had to shrug off discouragement, because I watched my classmates move up into more advanced sessions, while I still chased my dog.

That first summer slipped into the next, and still we drove to the field and attempted to complete full courses with some degree of accuracy. We took classes and tried to emulate all those capable members of the club. We learned how to complete a pinwheel, a series of jumps placed in a circle. Daisy learned to look for me when she blasted out of a tunnel, to see where to go next. And her self-control began to surface, so she didn't dash off for a dip in the pond during every run.

Daisy learned to do each obstacle—the teeter totter, the tall, narrow dog walk, the peaked A-frame, tunnels, broad jumps and even snaking through the weave poles. She began to wait for me at the bottom of the contact equipment (teeter, walk and A-frame), instead of launching off into the wild blue yonder alone. I began to learn handling techniques—where and when to cross in front of or behind my dog, how to cue her in time for the next obstacle, and to keep my hands where she could see them. But the magic would come when we could put it all together and work as a team.

Daisy thrived on the sensory stimulation and physical activity. I began to relax, make friends, and benefit from the good exercise. Most of the club members and students were women, and a surprising number of them were over fifty. One of them, Julie, proclaimed that she thought agility would prevent Alzheimer's disease.

"It's true!" she announced, and we all laughed. "You have to run and stay physically fit, use your mind to train your dog, memorize courses, socialize with friends, and you're playing with your dog outdoors. It's the perfect prescription!" We agreed, happy to have anything validate our obsession or, as some say, addiction.

Ever so gradually, Daisy and I developed some consistency in our work together. We began to have some very successful practice rounds. When we worked together, and Daisy understood my proper and timely cues, it felt like dancing. It really did, and we celebrated with well-deserved hugs and splendid rewards—cheese, smoked turkey and special liver treats for Daisy, and pure, joyful satisfaction and pride for me.

Walter captured some of our best moments on the field with his camera. A particularly handsome shot of Daisy, trotting with confidence across the dog walk, displayed her beauty and personality. This photo earned her the title of Miss June and a place in the La Plata Humane Society's 2007 calendar, a tribute to some of their most successful adoptions.

I'd always laughed off any thought or inquiry about competition. I'm not naturally athletic or competitive, and so far, our agility experiences had been more comedic than successful. But my classmates began to talk about going to an actual, real, sanctioned agility trial. They urged me to consider it. We discussed what it would be like, how embarrassing it could be, how much fun to go together, and finally decided to take the plunge. Ready or not, our gang—self-dubbed The Wild Bunch, for obvious reasons—filled out entry forms and committed to go to Moab, Utah to a NADAC, the North American Dog Agility Council, trial. We wondered what it would be like to earn our first Qs—qualifying runs that would lead to titles. While none of us expected to get any, we all secretly hoped for beginner's luck to strike. I wrote the following account for the club newsletter.

Newbies at the Start Line
Dedicated to all those who have gone before,
and those who still dream of the start line.

After two summers of classes, two winters of intermittent practice and lots of angst, The Wild Bunch decides to enter their first trial. Those in the know say the Moab NADAC fun-raiser is a great place to start, so entries are sent, gear is packed, and the gang speeds off to put their dogs and themselves to the test. The play opens as Holli and Gay depart for Moab.

"Just Getting There"
"How can there be so much stuff for just two people and two dogs for two nights?" Gay asks, as we survey the heap of bags, gear, water and food piled in her driveway.

"You never know what we might need," I warn. We stuff every recess of my Yukon, load the dogs into their crates and, taking a deep breath, the first of many, hit the road.

We left early, so we wouldn't be late for something or anything or because we were wound up like tops. We cruise along and Gay reads aloud from the NADAC rulebook. "It says here 'at the novice level, the dog is asked to perform the obstacles at a moderate distance.' What do you think 'moderate' is? And here it says, 'you and your dog are expected to move as a fast-moving, smooth-functioning team.' Do we know how to do that? What if we screw up?" The questions are endless and the answers elusive.

"Have we actually done that?" I ask.

We look at each other and choke in unison: "Aacckk!"

We pull in at 1:00 p.m. and spot the trial site, a large horse arena just off the highway. We're eager to secure our spot, get set up, and walk the dogs around a couple of times. Okay, we want to spend the next ten hours there, so the dogs can get settled. There's not a car in sight, and the desert wind sighs all around us.

"Maybe everyone is parked in back," Gay says, bright as usual. We pull around to see only NADAC chair Sharon's big RV, disabled and being repaired. A dirt-smudged man emerges from beneath the behemoth.

"Yeah, she's inside," he drawls in a southern accent.

We approach her door tentatively, not wanting to put a foot wrong before we even get started. We exchange pleasantries and she tells us we can set up after 4:00 p.m. today.

"Oh, good!" we gush, as eager as puppies seeking attention. We trundle off to town to check in at the motel and begin to sort gear. It seems to have increased in quantity and volume during the drive. We could outfit a small retail store, just from the back of the Yukon.

Four o'clock arrives, and so do we at the arena. A lone car sits outside. All the doors are closed. We panic that we've missed a tiny window of set-up time.

No, we're just very, very early, yet again. Hyperventilating, we dash from door to door, finally finding one open. Trial helpers work inside, sorting a mountain of water bags that need filling for tunnel anchors. Can we help?

"You bet!" we crow, heaving to like Girl Scouts working for a badge.

After filling, hauling and stacking forty tons of water, we ask for more. "That's all," we're told. "And it's okay to set up on that side, in the corner, not too close, not too far, in just the right spot." Oh, dear — what if we do it wrong? "Aacckk!" we croak.

"My God, It's Trial Day!"

Since this is a casual fun-raiser, there's nothing in writing about the day's schedule, the run down of classes or anything about when, where or how to be a good participant. We feel like we're winging it, big time. Not wanting to overwhelm our dogs or ourselves, we've registered for just one class the first day. Afraid to be late, we arrive at 8:00 a.m. We spend the next eight hours pacing, sitting, snacking and dog walking before our class that, of course, turns out to be the last one of the day.

With each course revision, we pop from our seats, stare like deer in the headlights, and ask, "What's happening?!" We spin to face each other and, bug-eyed, chirp, "Are we up next?!" No, it's not our turn, and the panic subsides. Twenty minutes later, the scene plays out again, and again.

Huddled together like a brood of motherless chicks, the Wild Bunch has converged on one side of the arena, while the more experienced competitors lounge calmly on the other side. Some even read books, and their dogs doze quietly. It's a marked contrast to the perpetual motion in Newbie Camp, where everyone watches to see what we should be doing or not doing.

During the day, a few of the braver newbies actually run their dogs. Miraculously, they survive to tell the tale to those of us still breathless on the sidelines. Remember, we've been hyperventilating for hours. We sideline folk cheer lustily for every newbie who ventures forth and returns to camp. No matter the outcome, we cheer. We've seen each other's struggles for two years and believe in our souls that just being here is tantamount to a splendid, soaring victory.

Kathy discovers that winter training has paid off, and she's now running Archer the Fast Dog, formerly Archer the Intelligent or the Distracted, but only sometimes the Focused. They complete runs in record time for them and the crowd goes wild. Well, Newbie Camp anyway.

Christine, not a true newbie, but sitting with the others and just as nervous, has brought her two female Aussies to compete. Today, she can run only Mocha, since Sera has gone into heat overnight. During several runs, Mocha exhibits her preference for contacts, whether they're part of the run or not, becoming the only dog there with "contact suck." She also draws attention to herself by rambling among the obstacles and finally relieving herself in the middle of the course. Christine is mortified, and carries Mocha outside.

Four o'clock arrives and so does our one and only run of the day, a novice jumpers course. Ellen has kindly offered to walk it with us and coach us along. Hearts pounding, we step out, getting the lay of the land. And guess what? It's not so hard. Eric has had us doing far more difficult courses in class, so we're relieved and actually believe we can do it.

Gay and Zeke take their place at the start line. With a nod from the timer, they dash off to the first jump. They finish the course with only a few miscues.

"How'd we do?" Gay asks, claiming amnesia for the entire course.

We're next up. I've been praying to my doggie angels (dearly departed goldens from my life, who are always there when I need them), and they've promised us a clean run. I remember what Daisy once told me: Expect the best. I do and we're off, Daisy actually following my directions, coming back to me when she strays — that's very big for Daisy — and sure enough, it was a clean run. Hooray!

Suddenly, in less than a minute, we're no longer newbies, but new initiates. We've joined the club, didn't embarrass ourselves, and can't wait to do it again. Fortunately, there's tomorrow, and we've even added a class. Cool.

"Day Two — We Can Do This"

We saunter in at 8:30 a.m., knowing we don't run until later. We downplay our eagerness, now newly confident and settled in camp. We even visit with some of the elite handlers, who actually speak to us — wow! It's a new day and we're on top of our game.

Today, we'll do three runs. After walking the course and feeling confident where to put every front and rear cross, Gay and Zeke tackle the Touch 'N Go course. Afterwards, Gay laments, "He didn't touch, he just went." He also almost "went" on one of those water bags, but was distracted in the nick of time. Tunnelers is more successful and, despite a wrong way tunnel, they finish with most of Gay's memory and Zeke's attention intact.

Daisy begins her first Touch 'N Go run like a rocket—through the first tunnel, the second tunnel, into the third tunnel. Then, I turn toward the teeter and experience a moment of hubris: I'm as fast as my dog, even faster because here I am next to the teeter and she's not quite here yet. Wait—I'm past the teeter and it hasn't moved. I spin around and see—nothing. There's no dog.

"Daisy!" I sing out. Nothing. I dash back toward my last sighting of her. "Daisy?" Nothing.

"Yoo hoo!" I warble, and a golden head pops up from a pen outside the course. Her expression says, "Oh, right, we were doing something," and she careens back onto the course. Undaunted, although already eliminated, I pick up where we left off, and she goes like a champ, never hesitating at new equipment, and occasionally adding a spin or twist for flourish. I'm thrilled, and the Wild Bunch cheers.

A fierce, hot wind howls outside the arena for most of the day, and some of us find pink sand dunes in our vehicles that we have left open. Somehow the grit there is a reminder of our own grit in getting started on this new course in our lives. It really is all about having fun with your dog, sharing the good times with like-minded friends, and taking a chance.

We did, and we wouldn't trade it for anything (except maybe a Q).

Many thanks to Eric, our patient and encouraging instructor, our mentors in DAD, our wonderful dogs, and all the rollicking, cheering support from the Wild Bunch. We had a blast.

Moving On, and On

We survived our first trial in Moab. Encouraged, Daisy and I struck out on the agility circuit. Sounds like we knew what we were doing, doesn't it? While there are at least five different trial sanctioning organizations, I decided to stick with NADAC, and later added AKC events. NADAC courses tend to be longer, loopier and easier for my long-legged girl to use her big stride between obstacles. AKC courses are tighter, considered more technical, require greater skill of both dog and handler, and sometimes it's harder for Daisy to make those turns. So, for now, it was NADAC.

Following the guidance of our more experienced club members (which was just about everyone else), Gay and I began to plan our next trial experiences. One of the trials that received raves in the past was held indoors at a horse arena in Penrose, Colorado. The arena was supposed to be nice, even sporting a small restaurant that served good food. Located somewhere near Canon City, it seemed to be at the end of the Pony Express route, but we decided to give it a try.

The way Colorado drives go, the four-hour trip was easy, with only two high altitude passes. We arrived mid-afternoon the day before the trial opened. Gay spotted the arena, in the middle of very deserted, dry, dusty acreage a mile or so outside of town. A couple of cars were parked by the east entrance, so we turned in there. After we walked the dogs and returned them to the Yukon, we opened the door.

The arena had fallen into a severe state of disrepair. It looked like no one had set foot inside for months, even years. We walked inside, and our hearts sank. We were going to spend a full weekend in this God-forsaken place? There were no lights on. We later learned the power had been turned off when bills weren't paid. The surface of the arena had petrified into rock-hard, rutted ground. It hadn't seen a piece of tilling or dragging equipment since forever. It looked like a twisted ankle or dog's wrenched knee waiting to happen. The cobwebs had cobwebs. Filth and despair had settled permanently on all the rusted metal rails, grandstand seats and the oh, so abandoned café and kitchen upstairs.

Gay and I wandered in disbelief.

"Is this it?" Gay whispered to me, not wanting to disturb the ghosts haunting the premises.

"Must be." I tried to wrap my head around what we'd gotten ourselves into.

"We don't have to stay," Gay offered, serving up the brightest thought we could muster.

"You're right."

Just then, a couple of the local host club members emerged out of the cloak of darkness.

"Hi!" they both said, as they smiled at us. "Welcome to our trial. We sure hope you have a good time. Let us know if we can answer any questions."

"Thanks." Their cheerfulness was a stark contrast to the grim, funereal atmosphere.

"Okay," Gay said, *sotto voce* to me. "We can come tomorrow morning, and if it's really dreadful, we can leave by noon."

I nodded. "We could stop in Salida and have a nice lunch at Laughing Ladies and shop a bit. We could walk the dogs by the river." Anywhere else was better than here.

We dropped off our dog crates and ground cloth and just a few things for our "campsite" for the next day. We wanted to keep our departure options open. We left little, so we could pack up fast.

The motel wasn't too bad, and there seemed to be a couple of satisfactory restaurants nearby. We learned that most of the visitors to Penrose were probably there to see inmates at the nearby state penitentiary in Canon City. Great. All this and prison, too. We observed a number of those probable visitors in the motel parking lot, some doing engine repair on a big truck, others hanging nearby, smoking and generally creating a rather unsavory atmosphere. Things were going downhill, and it was only 3:00 PM.

Other DAD members arrived and shared our shock and horror at the arena condition.

"I swear, it wasn't like this last time I was here," Cindy, one of those who had extolled the virtues of this trial, said. "If it had looked like this, I never would have suggested it, let alone come myself."

We hauled a big Chinese meal back to our room, and shared it with our group. We speculated on what tomorrow might bring, shook our heads, and settled in for the night.

When we arrived early the next morning, things looked a bit better. More people showed up and the members of the host club were knocking themselves out to overcome the deficits of the venue. We learned that the arena owners had fallen on hard times, and the arena followed suit. With no alternative location, the club decided to persevere. Porta potties were set up outside. They brought in huge submarine sandwiches at noon, followed by several big sheet cakes in the afternoon. Club members went overboard to welcome us and compensate for the arena's lack of everything with their good cheer and hard work.

Even the judge helped to turn the tide. Dwayne was a big man of substantial proportions, an air traffic controller from New Jersey by day and a NADAC judge on weekends. He was suffering from a bad back, no doubt aggravated by hours on a plane to get here. Still, his good spirits shone like a beacon in the darkness.

"Welcome everyone," he boomed in the echoing cavern. "I know things may not be quite what you expected, but we're going to make the best of it and have a good time anyway." He was a man of his word—we were going to make lemonade out of lemons.

Dwayne's big persona and cheerful demeanor filled the space. He complimented each team, no matter how difficult a run they'd experienced. He thanked every one of us who volunteered to work on the ring crew. I pledged to go out of my way to attend any trial he judged.

Gay and I remained for the whole weekend, truly enjoyed it, had a few nice runs, and avoided injury to our dogs and ourselves. But it's unlikely we'll ever return there.

At the other end of the spectrum is the Fiesta Cluster Show in Scottsdale, Arizona, at the immense, sprawling Westworld Equestrian Center. After I enjoyed several other small venues in Albuquerque, Phoenix and Durango, I took the plunge and entered the AKC show in Scottsdale.

Just getting there in late February proved a challenge. It snowed heavily as Walter and I worked our way south and back into sunshine. We set up Daisy's crate, my chair and some other ringside essentials and surveyed our surroundings.

Sprawled over many acres, this show included everything we'd seen in Denver, but even more of it. All the events were set on thick, luxurious green grass. Vendors' tents covered parking lot areas, and hundreds of RVs parked cheek to jowl on all sides. Massive vehicles of professional handlers nosed toward the conformation rings. Smaller, more modest RVs and trailers settled on the outskirts. Golf carts were available to rent by the day for the "commute" to ringside campsites. I was overwhelmed and wondered if Daisy and I had bitten off more than we could chew. Chatter, on the other hand, was just beginning in agility and wasn't ready yet for a trial. She'd get to spend lots of one-on-one time with Walter.

Over the four-day event, we had some nice runs and even garnered some Qs. The weather was perfect and Daisy enjoyed the hubbub. Four agility rings ran concurrently, so I had to stay on my toes to know when we had to be where. One run on a jumpers course stands out in my mind. Daisy loves these courses that are mostly jumps over hurdles and was absolute perfection throughout, until I sent her over a wrong jump just at the end. My mistake! The crowd had been cheering us on, and then groaned in unison, as I collapsed on the grass in disbelief. But Daisy was thrilled, bounced on top of me, and reminded me that it was all about the journey, rather than the destination. I still remember that as one of our finest partnerships—until I let my girl down and guided her over the wrong jump. But then, it's usually the handler's fault.

Except for a run the next day. Daisy was overjoyed to see so many of her fans again at ringside. Throughout the run, she ventured over to say hello, thank them for coming, and flip her golden locks provocatively. She did complete a few obstacles, but the lure of her fan base was too seductive. Fame had gone to her head.

By the last day, I was exhausted. In a stupor, I sat next to Daisy and watched a group of people walk a course. *Funny, those were the same people who had been in most of our other classes during the weekend. Wait—maybe that's our next class.* I sprang from my lethargy to check the list of entrants on the board. We were supposed to run next, but I was far too late and unprepared. I scratched us from the class and decided it was time to pack it in. Once again, handler error.

Agility According to Daisy

If Daisy were a student in a classroom, she'd sit in the front row, shoot her hand in the air to answer every question, grin when she's right (and look around to see that everyone else noticed), shrug off errors, and seize every day as if it were Christmas morning.

With that kind of chutzpah, it seems only fair that she get to share some thoughts and opinions, and boy, she's got 'em.

Daisy here, folks. Mom wanted me to let you know what I think of agility, and how I approach a course. Sure thing—you betcha! So let's get going, from when mom walks out on a course and leaves me at the start line.

Oh, boy! Another run on the course! I sure do love this stuff! Ooops—you want me where? Is this better? Hurry up—let's GO! It's hard for me to wait, while she walks out on the course, but I've gotten pretty darned good at it, if I do say so myself. She knows she

can really rely on me here. I'm not taking my eyes off
her now — we're almost ready, and — here we go!

There's a jump, now here comes the dog walk —
this is okay, but she wants me to slow down here at
the end — I'm still not sure what she wants now —
speed or that funny "slow" thing she asks for?

No matter — we're still doin' okay — now what
does she want? When she's not clear, it's dang hard
for me to know. I wish she'd keep her hand lower, so
I could see it better. There — that's just right — Okay,
I'm into the tunnel — now what? Okay, it's the tire —
wheee — I'm flyin'!

Ooops, I kinda skidded there, but we're back on
track. Three jumps in a row — my best thing. And
now the A-frame — that's my very favorite — and I
love to launch off at the end — oooff, just like that.
Now around to another tunnel — boy, I hope she's
out there, 'cause it's hard to know where to go when
I come blasting out. Oh, good — she's pointing to
the — what? Where? Okay, now to the weaves. Ooops,
I must've missed one. Back to the beginning — did I
mess up again? Okay, here we go — 1, 2, 3, 4, 5, 6, 7, 8,
9, 10 and I'm out. Ooops again? Oh, well, I'll hit it next
time.

Off we go to the teeter. This used to scare me, but
I've got it nailed now, even including that "dirt" thing
at the end. Bang goes the end and I'm spot on. Okay,
a pinwheel — that's three jumps in a circle — easy for
her, harder for me. Now here's a switch — I love that!
Spot on again, changing direction and never missed
a beat. Now three jumps in a row — she says "Go on!"
and boy, do I! Across the finish line — now that was

a blast, wasn't it?! Here come my treats — oooh, that good cheese stuff. She seems pretty happy, but says we have some things to work on. Yippee — more courses!

One year, before the DAD club put on an agility trial over Labor Day, mom asked me a few questions. She said she wanted to post something each day for everybody at the trial. So, this is what we said to each other.

Saturday's Words
from
Conversations with My Dog
by Holli Pfau (person)
and Daisy Pfau (golden retriever)

D: Why are you so slow?

H: Because I only have two legs. And I'm old.

D: How old are you?

H: In dog years, I'm three times your age.

D: Wow. And you can still run.

H: Yup. Amazing, isn't it?

Sunday's Words

D: When do I get to make up the course?

H: Never.

D: How come I don't get extra credit for spinning and twirling around obstacles?

H: Because that's not part of the plan.

D: Why can't I jump in the pond or the ditch during a run?

H: Same reason.

D: Chase birds?

H: Same.

D: Catch ducks?

H: Not on the menu.

D: Roll in stuff?

H: Don't even think about it.

D: Stop to smell the...

H: Do it on your own time.

Monday's Words

D: Why do you do agility?

H: Because it looked like fun, playing together, getting exercise, learning new things, hanging out with other people and dogs. Why do you do it?

D: Because you asked me to dance. And I said yes.

A Change in Plans

Before I entered the hospital via the emergency room on a Thursday, I called Gay and left a message. "Gay, I don't think I'll be going with you to Grand Junction this weekend for the trial," I said matter-of-factly. "I'm in the ER and waiting to hear what's going on."

How could this be? I pondered, stretched out in my hospital bed. An IV trickled fluid into my arm. The clock on the wall ticked minutes into hours. Just a week before, Gay and I had been chief ring stewards at the DAD Labor Day trial. We managed many of the behind the scenes elements of the trial, including coordinating volunteer workers for every class for three days. One evening, we stood by Gail, who suddenly had to put her aged dog to sleep. The next morning, we were back at the trial. And somehow, we managed to run our dogs, earn some Qs, and not collapse under the load.

But now, weak and wondering what my diagnosis was, I awaited test results.

It wasn't good news. A tumor was bleeding in my stomach, and surgery was the only treatment. While we made plans to travel to the Mayo Clinic in Scottsdale, my condition worsened and my options evaporated.

"Shall I ask the surgeon to come in?" The gastroenterologist had monitored my deteriorating status Sunday afternoon.

"Yes, I guess so." Suddenly my health and future were in the hands of a man I'd never met.

Our new $85 million, eighty-two-bed Mercy Regional Medical Center hospital was completed earlier in the summer. I toured during pre-opening days when community members were invited to visit every unit of the facility, including the operating rooms. I admired the beautiful patient rooms and the handsome and carefully selected original artwork. Our small community was fortunate to have such state-of-the-art medical care right at home. I felt grateful that I wouldn't need their services for a long time. I was wrong.

The surgeon arrived, reviewed my case, and outlined his plan. He was just the right combination of comforting bedside manner and businesslike competence. I felt more comfortable and resigned myself to surgery as soon as it could be scheduled.

Walter had taken me to the ER four days before and we tried to piece together what the results of many tests meant. He faithfully shuttled the half hour between home and hospital several times each day, to comfort me and also care for the dogs. Gay and Gail jumped in to assist with their feeding schedule and outdoor runs.

The next afternoon, one of the nurses who directs the TLC (Touch, Love and Compassion) program arrived in my room. This special, holistic support service employs many non-traditional therapies, like therapeutic touch, guided imagery, aromatherapy and meditation. Janet provided me with a CD to use in preparation for surgery, music to take into the operating room and a lavender-scented eye pillow. She also asked me some interesting questions.

"Do you have guiding spirits that are a source of strength and comfort to you?" she asked in a gentle voice.

"Absolutely!" I said. "I call upon the spirits of four wonderful golden retrievers who were so important in my life, and they continue to be there for me from the other side."

"Ah, good." She smiled, recognizing someone who believes in angels and spiritual help that is often beyond full human comprehension.

"They're already here with me," I said. The four had come to my side immediately on admission, and had remained close at hand. The author of a book on angels says that angels like to be invited in, asked for help, and given a task. I'd done that for sure, and my golden guiding lights hadn't disappointed me.

"Keep them nearby and rely on them," Janet reminded me, and she promised to return during my hospitalization.

For the next two days, I felt my already low energy ebb further away. I did my homework, listened to the CD, practiced visualizations, and sought comfort from my golden guides. I let my mind settle into peacefulness. Nik always sat by my left shoulder. Older, wiser and probably a very senior kind of angel, she seemed to direct the others. Bodie pulled himself away from some deep wilderness to hover on my right side, a bit uncertain, but here in stalwart support. Newer at this guardian angel business, Sophie and Tucker sat by my feet, taking it all in, and learning the ropes.

The day for surgery arrived, and I was ready. Staff bustled in and out, to perform last minute tests. Mentally prepared, I was eager to move ahead. But at the last minute, my turn on the table was postponed for a day. My doctor had an emergency gall bladder surgery to perform, and I was re-scheduled.

"Worse luck," I reported to Walter when he arrived. "I got bumped by a gall bladder. But it's oddly comforting to know that they thought my condition was less serious and I could wait."

Interesting. Just like we had to postpone Tucker's hip surgery for two weeks.

The next morning, I was more than ready. "I hear the theme from *Rocky*," I told Walter, with what little spunk I had left. "Let's get this show on the road!"

When the green-clad nurses and staff wheeled me into the operating room, I knew I wasn't alone. The nurses saw just one sedated woman on the gurney, but I had much more company than that.

I could feel them, right there beside me—Nikki, Bodie, Sophie and Tucker. I could almost hear the click of their nails on the floor, feel their breath against my cheek, touch their silken fur.

Surgery went smoothly, post-op pain was well managed, and the attentive staff cared for all my needs. Some days were harder than others, and I was especially grateful to see Su-zanne, one of Janet's colleagues, on one of those days. She swaddled my chilled body in warm blankets, snuggled my head in a hot towel, and left me listening to a soothing CD, while I inhaled a rosemary fragrance. That day, my golden guides stayed very close at hand. I also saw my two current girls and even my equine soul mate at bedside. While some of that vision may have been drug-induced, I was nonetheless grateful for their supportive energy. They were a comfort and I'm sure the source of great healing powers.

I began to walk the prescribed laps around the unit, towing an IV pole, many bags of fluids and other less pleasant tubes in different orifices. I pushed every day to increase the number of laps, as if they would earn me my ticket home. It worked.

After thirteen days of a very unanticipated experience, I was wheeled outside into the crisp glare of a September afternoon. I squinted in the bright sun, while Walter and the nurse carefully tucked me into the front seat of the Yukon. I was headed home.

We'd already discussed how I could interact with the rambunctious girls. I'd get settled upstairs and remain there for the next several days and not even attempt to go up and down the stairs to the living room or kitchen. Walter, bless him, would bring my meals up to me. He'd also escort each girl on a tightly controlled leash in to see me, while I sat in a chair, with a double pillow barrier between their energy and my tender incision.

The dogs were beside themselves with joy, and it was hard to contain their enthusiasm. I tried to absorb their energy right through my hands, as I hugged them, caressed their beautiful coats, and assured them I was home for good. I only had enough energy for a few minutes of their welcome, but I knew how therapeutic this would be. They linked me to another level of the spiritual world and would nurture my return to health in a way nothing else could.

I'd lost a lot of weight—not eating for two weeks will do that for you—some muscle strength and certainly stamina. The first week slipped past me like a silent, dense fog. I ate tiny portions of simple foods, got to see my dogs, mindlessly watched whatever was on TV, and slept a lot. Ever so gradually, my strength began to return and I was permitted to rejoin the family downstairs. It was the first step toward getting my independence back, and it felt wonderful. Who knew that padding around the kitchen in robe and slippers, heating soup, and having my girls close by could feel so fabulous?

Gay and Gail had been the point people for keeping my friends advised of my progress. Gail's husband Norman, a retired ophthalmologist, had sat with us at the hospital for many hours, talked with my doctors, and helped to interpret information for us. People from DAD and my other community affiliations sent many cards and flowers. Friends arrived with chicken noodle soup, squash soup and custard. It was all therapeutic and I was on my way toward full recovery.

My fall agility trial schedule had been cancelled, but I began to think about when I'd be able to run again with Daisy. Gay pestered me when she thought I could take the pressure. "So—shall I sign us up for Phoenix in January? How about Denver in February?"

I hesitated. "I just don't know. Give me another few weeks to decide."

"Okay. But the closing dates for entries are coming up and we don't want to miss out."

Recovery and progress are never linear, and I experienced ups and downs. I learned that the tumor had been malignant, but was excised with clean margins, along with a third of my stomach. I was referred into a clinical trial for an oral chemotherapy drug and started that protocol. I tolerated the drug well for the forty-eight-week course of treatment and could resume activities during that time. My energy ebbed and flowed, and running flat out on a course beside my dog seemed very far away. But in the end, it was my commitment to Daisy and our agility career that was probably the strongest force propelling me forward.

I began to take walks, then go with Daisy to the field, then do a couple of obstacles together. Maybe a trial was possible after all.

Phoenix marked my return to one of the things I loved most. We went, we ran, and we did okay. But for some reason, I remember the big Denver show in mid-February as the real marker of my recovery.

Gay had to bow out of this trip, but I decided to journey forth alone. In the middle of a snowy week, Daisy and I departed from Durango, to caravan behind good friends and fellow DAD members Diane and Betty. All went fine for the first couple of hours, and then, we hit Wolf Creek Pass. At ten thousand feet, this pass and its homey little ski area receive more snow than any other place in Colorado, and that's saying a lot. This day, it looked to me like they could get a good share of their annual total. The snow fell thickly, the wind whirled and whipped, and I could barely see Diane's white Jeep in front of me. Despite plows that worked up and down both sides of the pass, there must have been half a foot of fresh powder on the road. We both slowed to a crawl and crept over the summit, held our breaths and prayed for divine guidance. Our dogs slept soundly in the back of our cars, oblivious to the harrowing drive.

By the time we reached Walsenburg, night was falling, the storm felt deep and heavy on our shoulders, and we decided to bivouac at the next motel. Nice rooms awaited us, the owner welcomed our dogs, and the adjacent diner served passable meals, a huge plus since we weren't driving another inch that night. We walked our dogs in the deep white stuff and bedded down early.

By morning, another foot of snow blanketed the ground, but the sun was trying to stage a comeback. Glad that we'd allowed an extra day for this trip, we loaded up and prepared to head north, but Diane's car wouldn't start. After several hours of problem solving and the help of the local auto parts store and a couple of motel workers, a new starter motor let us resume the journey.

We sailed along for several hours, until we approached the outskirts of Denver. Once again, blowing snow reduced visibility, and by then, we were ensnared in four o'clock traffic on the freeways, trying to reach the show site. Staying in touch by cell phone, Betty kept calling me with navigation details. Just as we approached a tricky interchange, my cell rang again.

"Holy crap!" I answered, knowing it would be Betty. "I can't see a thing!" She laughed, gave me the right exit info, and I sighed in relief to be on surface streets, even if they were slick.

We set up our camp inside the arena, sloshed through the mud and muck in the parking lot, and then settled into our motel. Tomorrow would be a busy day for all of us. Experienced travelers, all of our dogs took everything in stride.

Only five months past surgery, I hoped I had the stamina for this strenuous event. Competitors are on their feet all day long, walking dogs outside, walking courses inside, and then running with their dogs. In addition to agility, I'd also entered Daisy in rally obedience that was held upstairs in the building across the parking lot. It was a full dance card and I hoped I was up for it. Daisy certainly was.

I wish I'd worn a pedometer that weekend. Who knows how many miles I walked, how many flights of stairs I climbed, and how much energy I burned, preparing for all these events? But somehow, I was buoyed by the mere fact of being there.

The first morning, as we waited for our turn in the agility ring, I felt lots of nervous energy all around me. I paused to watch teams line up to run. All the handlers seemed tight and tense, and the dogs seemed to absorb that twittering emotion.

Me? I was just counting my blessings. "We get to be here!" I proclaimed to Daisy, who danced at my side. "We get to be here!" I stopped outside the ring and looked up at the tiers of seats filled with spectators, and remembered how Gay, Gail and I had felt just a year ago, watching others run courses. And now, here I was, ready or not, stepping into a space I never would have thought possible.

"Daisy girl," I said, looking deeply into her twinkling eyes, "We're lucky just to be here. That's our prize, and that's all I could hope for."

Daisy sparkled, revved and ready to run. "Expect the best," she smiled back up at me. In the midst of all that swirled around us, we were a team and grateful for this day.

During the weekend, we earned a couple of Qs, had a lot of fun runs, cheered and celebrated with our friends, and slept like logs at night. Each day, we trotted over to the quiet oasis of the obedience rings to await our turn to impress the judges with our rally moves. With lots of practice and good coaching from Mary, Daisy had truly blossomed into a rally star. She'd learned how to channel her enthusiasm and performed our courses as if we were dancing. She pranced her way through every task at this show and earned her Rally Excellent title with three consecutive stellar performances.

Bursting with pride, she and I returned to the agility arena after our achievement. I cradled a two-foot long, slender pewter dish with her title ribbons inside and bounced toward our DAD encampment. "Look!" I proclaimed to her friends, who surrounded us, heaped praise on Daisy's head, and flung hugs around my shoulders. "We did it! She was awesome!"

The ribbons were great, the prizes a bonus, and our teamwork praiseworthy. But the most treasured memory of our experience was just being there. It was a gift unlike anything I could imagine. They say cancer changes you, puts everything in perspective, and sifts away the chaff. It does, and it heightens your awareness of what is truly important in your life. Those four days with Daisy are gems I treasure.

The next year, Gay joined me on a return trip to the scene of so much success. We had the usual smorgasbord of runs—some great, some marginal and a few downright laughable. One afternoon, Daisy and I were in the midst of a comedic routine. She was just too distracted to focus and kept spinning with excitement. When I directed her into a tunnel, I lost my footing and landed smack on my butt, right at the start of the tunnel. Daisy bounced as if to say, "Oh, boy! Mom's right here on the ground next to me!"

I scrambled to my feet, with Daisy still atop me. "Daisy! Go tunnel! Go on!" She sped through and finished the course with a flourish. There was nothing I could do but laugh and hug her. What a silly run!

"Excuse me," the polite woman said to us, just outside the

ring. "I'm with *The Denver Post* and I wonder if I could talk with you about your run?"

"Sure, why not?" I laughed. *Now why couldn't she have seen our flawless jumpers run earlier that day?*

The next morning, Daisy and I made the Monday paper. Here's what the reporter wrote:

"Daisy was having a 'ditsy blond' day.

The golden retriever couldn't stay focused, stopping halfway through the weaves to dash toward the jump. Her handler, Holli Pfau of Durango, smiled and called her back.

'She had a perfect run on the weaves the other day,' said Pfau. 'Sometimes, she's just a ditsy blond.'"

The article about the whole show concluded with this:

"For Daisy and Pfau, winning is nice, but even on the ditsy runs, it's about having fun.

'It's like dancing with Fred Astaire when it's good,' she said. 'But, even though it wasn't a qualifying run, we had a blast.'"

The National!

In early 2007, I began to consider attending the Golden Retriever National Specialty Show in Snohomish, Washington, north and east of Seattle. It would be a wonderful way to mark one year since surgery. We could visit Jenny and Margo, and also stop by some of our favorite places along the way. I started to make plans.

Excited by all that was offered on the Golden Retriever Club of America's (GRCA) website, I signed up for everything we could enter: rally, agility, the rescue parade, a freestyle workshop and a big dinner. I arranged to rent a trailer that would be set up on site, so I could enjoy the atmosphere. Over twelve hundred dogs were entered in the various events. I couldn't imagine being surrounded day and night by so many golden retrievers—all those fluffy, gorgeous coats, the ear-to-ear grins, and infectious *joie de vivre* attitudes.

We purchased a small cargo trailer to haul all the supplies we'd need for three weeks on the road. We could stash everything in the trailer and keep the back of the Yukon spacious for the dogs and a few necessities like jackets, water and lunch.

Walter, Daisy, Chatter and I departed for the 1,255-mile drive north and west. Seasoned travelers by now, the girls rode well, pulled eagerly on leashes during leg-stretching walks for all of us, and each night settled like veterans into new hotel surroundings. Salt Lake City, Utah; Boise, Idaho; Hermiston and Astoria, Oregon—we gained ground daily and also enjoyed the sights. A walk along the banks of the robust Columbia River was a feast for the senses for the girls—seagulls, ships, walkers, water and noses full of fresh air. But walk as we did, nothing could take the place of a good off-leash romp. I knew they were building storehouses of unspent energy.

We arrived at the show site mid-afternoon, the Harvey Airfield in Snohomish. The sprawling acres of thick, green grass buzzed with activity as local volunteers set up show rings, erected huge white tents, marked grids for RV sites, and strung electrical outlets, while people exercised their goldens. I felt like I'd made a pilgrimage to the homeland and, flushed with excitement, jumped into the fray. We located our assigned site, unhitched the cargo trailer, and awaited delivery of our accommodation trailer. Once situated, we drove into Snohomish, a small town of art galleries and antique shops, with a few restaurants scattered on the quaint main street. We shopped for groceries and returned to the trailer to set up housekeeping. The girls were thrilled to be out of the car, and we walked miles around the site to get the lay of the land. The day was clear and sunny, and we hoped blue skies would last well into the week.

The next day dawned, but not clear. Fog settled over the valley and didn't lift until mid-morning. Our spirits undampened, the girls and I made our way around the huge field, to visit vendors set up on the perimeter and staffers at administrative tables in the main tent. I snatched up some early souvenirs and returned in time to greet Jenny, who arrived to spend the next three days camped out with me, while Walter took off for a photographic safari in Olympic National Park. He loves to explore wilderness areas that offer opportunities and challenges for his landscape photography. Crashing surf, rocky coastlines and lush rainforests lured him to the Olympic Peninsula.

"Isn't this wonderful?" Jenny crowed, taking in the sight. "This is going to be so much fun, just us and the dogs." She hugged me and the girls and bounced with excitement. Her thick, short-cropped hair was already curling in the dampness. It suits her enthusiastic personality.

Over the years, Jenny and her husband Dave have owned seven goldens, starting with Saffron, one of the first dogs in the PAT program. Like us, they've supported the work of rescue, and five of their goldens were either rescues or secondhand dogs. After they moved to Washington state in 1992, Jenny continued to volunteer with animal-assisted therapy programs and work with Delta Society, a Seattle-based organization that promotes the human-animal bond and establishes standards for animal-assisted therapy and activity programs. In 1997, her two dogs, Poppi and Roscoe, received Delta's Beyond Limits Award as Therapy Animals of the Year. She's a golden fan through and through, and a dear friend, colleague and confidant since 1987.

That day, my first event was scheduled, the agility trial. The field was lush, the temperature cool, and I knew Daisy and I were up to the task. It was our kind of weather and high time that we got to stretch our legs.

While we warmed up on the sidelines, Daisy pranced and beamed her "Let's get on with it!" expression up at me. We lined up and were off.

And off and off she went. "Daisy—here!" I called, as my exuberant wild child tore around the field. She tucked her little butt and ran even faster, spinning donuts around obstacles. Her eyes gleamed; her speed increased. Sure enough, six days of confinement in the car without a chance to rip had set her up for this rowdy runabout. The crowd around the ring laughed and cheered her on. It was obvious that there would be no Q on this course, so I let her run, grabbed a few obstacles when we could, and crossed the finish line to end this entertaining display. All good fun, but no cigar.

I could only laugh as I gathered her up and slipped a leash around her neck. Puffing only a little, Daisy was just warming up. I wondered if we'd made this long drive for naught. But we had two more runs ahead of us, so I walked off to spend some time re-focusing with her.

Next up was the FAST course. New in AKC agility this year, the obstacles on the course are set in a very angular fashion, the antithesis of smooth, flowing courses for jumpers or standard agility. Each obstacle is assigned a value, and the goal is to amass as many points as you can, in a sequence of your own design, before the timer goes off, indicating the end of your run. Truth be told, I liked the FAST classes, since they seemed to play to our strengths: speed and frequent inaccuracy. Daisy could take any obstacle, in almost any order, and we weren't penalized for erratic behavior. It was just our style.

"Okay, Daisy," I said, as we lined up at the start. "Let's see what we can do." Off we dashed, and she followed my cues, took obstacle after obstacle, racked up points, and moved with ease and grace. Apparently, the earlier rip was just enough to take the wild edge off, but not so much that she was fatigued. I pointed to the last three obstacles and the final jump. I hadn't heard the buzzer yet, so we were still on track. Just as she sailed over the last jump, the buzzer sounded. It was a perfect run, earned plenty of points, and used every split second of time we had available. "Hooray!" I cheered, and so did the crowd. Daisy loved it.

Our last run of the day was no less spectacular, and Daisy looked every inch the champ on a jumpers course, which is her favorite. I wonder if she enjoys the speed she can build, or the essence of flight when she springs over each jump? Today, she was perfection, and completed the course with a very fast time and no faults. More cheers at the end.

At the concluding ceremonies for the day, Daisy received two big first place ribbons and two special glass candle-holders, etched with "Goldens Make the World Go Around GRCA 2007." I could scarcely carry it all, and Jenny joined me to celebrate, with Chatter in hand. "I knew you could do it! Oh, Miss Daisy, you were quite the star today." Daisy grinned and soaked it all up.

Next morning, we got up early to be ready for an 8:00 AM start in rally and discovered we were enveloped in deep, thick fog that blanketed the entire site. Other handlers with their dogs emerged like ghosts from the dimness. Still and quiet, perhaps this atmosphere would help us focus on our task. Jenny and I dressed for a chilly day, with lots of layers, and headed out for the next adventure.

Daisy and Chatter were both entered, so we set up two crates at ringside, with our chairs, treats and snacks under our shade tent. Today, it might provide cover from rain instead. The sun struggled to break through the gloom, and handlers and their dogs began to work the course under the judge's watchful eye. Most teams performed competently, and I hoped this would bode well for us, too.

Daisy was already working for her RAE, Rally Advanced Excellent, the highest title in rally, so she needed to earn a passing score on both the advanced course and the excellent course, and then do it nine more times in future events. Chatter could earn her RE, Rally Excellent, title this day, so she'd have just one course to perform. I crossed my fingers and we began to strut our stuff.

Daisy was distracted by smells in the wonderful, deep grass, but I regained her attention before it was too late. At the end of the excellent course, she performed a perfect "back up three steps" in heel position, and the judge proclaimed it to be the best he'd seen all day. I thanked him for his kind comments, but we agreed that Daisy has other skills where she can improve. She passed both courses, although with lower than her usual stellar scores.

Chatter moved beautifully with me, paid attention, performed each station with care, and was a true partner in the exercise. She passed with high marks, earned her excellent title, and we celebrated in high style. Jenny had been sitting ringside, quietly sending us positive thoughts, and she reveled with us. The girls love Jenny and all four of us were jubilant with our success.

Later in the afternoon, just as the sun peeked out from the day's fog bank, Margo arrived to join the party. Margo has owned seven goldens and worked in Golden Rescue in Los Angeles in the 1980s. She and her first golden, the red-coated, mischievous, smiling Tangible were early members of PAT, until Margo, too, moved north to Washington. Margo and I met even before that, though, when I was a graduate advisor to our sorority at USC, and Margo was still in school. But our true connection has been the dogs, and we remain fast friends.

This evening was the highly touted Northwest Salmon Barbeque dinner under the big top tent. Margo knows many people in the world of conformation showing and fieldwork, and enjoyed catching up with them. Jenny and I browsed the art auction items and selected a table near the podium.

At the start of dinner, while people still settled down with their plates brimming from the buffet, Barbara came to the stage. This petite woman with short dark hair stepped confidently to the microphone. "Can I have your attention?" she demanded, over the din. "This is really important, so I need your attention now."

The hubbub died down, and she began an impassioned, articulate presentation on the need to raise $500,000 to donate to the Morris Foundation for cancer research. So many goldens now suffer and die from this horrible disease. GRCA will be able to help direct how these funds will be spent in cancer research.

"My husband and I have agreed that we will personally match every $100 donated with $5 of our own money. We're putting our money where my mouth is!"

While she continued to speak, a woman walked between the tables to hand her a $100 bill. Someone else came forward with a fist full of twenties. Someone else stepped up with a check in hand. The stream was constant, everyone eager to support the research needed to secure a more healthful future for our beloved dogs.

After dinner, we walked the girls around the field, admired other beautiful dogs, and enjoyed the evening. Daisy and Chatter relished this time outdoors, with people they love, doing what they enjoy. It had been a special day. Later, Jenny and I settled into our sleeping bags for a good night's sleep, before the next day's events. Margo returned home to care for her golden brood of three. She would return on the weekend.

The next morning, Jenny and I faced a new challenge: There was no water for showers, flushing or anything else. Despite our careful use of water from the trailer's tank, we couldn't muster more than a teaspoon from the tap. "No matter," Jenny said, brushing off the inconvenience. "We'll just fluff our hair, change our clothes, and look as good as new." Easy for her to say, Jenny of the thick, naturally curly, always perky salt-and-pepper gray coif.

"I bet we have enough bottled water to wash our hair in the sink," I offered, me of the fine, blonde do that needs shampooing and blow drying every day. We carefully dribbled our meager water supply over each other's heads, paused to shampoo, and just barely rinsed. A date with the dryer and we're good to go.

Today, the girls have no events scheduled, so we enjoyed a stroll with them around the grounds, stopped by the vendors, and made purchases. We watched splendid goldens compete in conformation. We visited with Barbara in the administrative tent and complimented her on her speech last night. People were still arriving at her desk to deliver donations.

We drove into Edmonds to seek out a knitting store. Jenny is a superb knitter, probably because she grew up in

New Zealand, the land of sheep and wool. I struggle, but always enjoy her tutoring, so I can improve my skills a bit. Afterwards, we headed to the harbor, for a seafood dinner overlooking Puget Sound.

"Today is the one year anniversary of my surgery," I announced to Jenny. "I can't think of a better way to celebrate recovery than being here for nationals with my friends." We toasted the occasion, and declared it the best reason ever to order dessert.

The next morning, we awakened again to fog, but embraced the muted scene and quiet start to the day. The girls peered through the gray to spot other dogs on leash, out for their morning constitutionals. Still without water, we rationed our bottled supply, and appreciated the porta potties nearby.

The entire day's activities today are dedicated to rescue. All donations to fund raising will be given to rescue. The highlight of events will be the Parade of Rescue Dogs during the noon lunch break in conformation judging. Daisy will be one of those dogs, so I spent a little extra time grooming her. She still has a rather thin coat for a golden, so it doesn't take long. Daisy is ready to go on a moment's notice, and today is no different.

The line-up began at 11:00 AM, as the fifty handlers checked in and received bandanas for their dogs, featuring red, orange and pink hearts. While I walked my girl among the throng of other teams, I saw great diversity. Dogs were young and old, as were their owners. Men, women and teenagers. Stunningly beautiful dogs and those with less than award-winning conformation. Red, blonde, silver and gold. Male and female. But one thing was constant: the grins on the faces of everyone on the grass, people and dogs alike. The atmosphere was celebratory: We were there to honor the lives of these dogs and the people who make rescue possible.

These dogs weren't competing in conformation, agility or obedience. They'd traveled from seven states to celebrate the most important achievement of all: survival. These dogs had been discarded, left by heartless humans at the edge of the road of life. And while their early months and years reflected hardship, they each now held a special place in the hearts of their families.

Today, they're rescued dogs, saved by dedicated volunteers with Golden Retriever Rescue organizations, shelters and humane societies. Where once their golden potential had been ignored and their loving hearts broken, now they flourish.

I paused on the outskirts of this scene. It occurred to me that without rescue, many of these dogs wouldn't be here at all. They wouldn't be anywhere. They would likely be dead. All these gorgeous, happy and joyful dogs, who now bring so much into the lives of their families, wouldn't have had a chance, except for the dedication of rescue volunteers.

At the top of that list are Nancy and Allan Kiesler, the chairs of the day's event. Over the loudspeaker, Nancy urged all the teams to line up by number and prepare for the parade. Daisy and I wore number thirty and we found our place. Daisy danced with excitement, and I felt proud to stand beside her.

A TV crew set up; spectators took their seats at ringside. A local TV news anchor stepped to the microphone. "Welcome ladies and gentlemen to our very special Parade of Rescue Dogs," she began. "I am also the lucky owner of a rescue dog, Kahlua. I'm happy to be here today to honor all of you."

One by one, she read the brief story of each dog, as the team circled around the ring to the applause of admiring onlookers. The dogs ranged in age from one-year-old Hannah to thirteen-year-olds Sandy Claws, Maize and Hunter. The stories were amazing. Here are just a few quotes from their bios:

> Maverick was given up by his owners after six years and he'd been left alone in the yard for a year and then turned in to a shelter.

> Leroy was just over four months old when the volunteers removed him, along with over two hundred other dogs, from a puppy mill.

> Mia came from a gentleman who had to move into assisted living.

> Hayden was found as a stray when he was about six months old.

> Ladybird was surrendered when her owners thought she might be pregnant.

> Sinjin was rescued when he was just five months old. He'd been abused and neglected.

> Hunter was rescued after being abandoned or lost in a rest area near the top of Mt. Hood, Oregon.

> Adopted at one year of age, Tarquin had spent most of her first year in an unlit garage.

Daisy's bio read like this:

> Renewing the licenses for my two goldens suddenly took an unexpected turn. Perusing my forms, the lady at the humane society took a shot in the not so dark: "Golden retrievers, I see. Would you like another?" Laughing, I said, "I always want another one." "We have a six-month-old female who was turned in an hour ago," she said, tempting me. Four days later, we picked up Daisy, a lean and wild flurry of frenetic motion. This little firecracker exploded into our lives, energetic and egocentric. With feet flying, tongue lolling and ears flopping, she tears through life at breakneck speed. A quick study, Daisy earned her rally excellent title in three straight days and competes in open AKC agility. At four, she is self-confident and approaching maturity—or so we hope!"

As Kathi shared Daisy's story with the crowd, Daisy and I took our turn in the ring. I wanted to show off some of her skills, so I cued her for a couple of fancy rally moves, including her recently lauded backing up in heel position. After we completed a couple of those, Daisy decided that the wet grass held more interest for her than what I asked, and she buried her nose in the lawn to inhale some mysterious, seductive smell. Not expecting this sudden stop, I was pulled backwards by the leash. I decided to go with the flow and pantomimed shock and surprise at this turn of events, and then we sprinted on, while the crowd laughed and clapped for Daisy Dog.

All the while, Jenny had shared Chatter's smile and her ever-present neediness with everyone who paused to be charmed by the little seductress. At one point, I looked over to see Chatter with her paws on Jenny's waist, while a cameraman filmed the two of them. Maybe that clip hit the airwaves in Seattle.

After the parade finished, special awards were presented to dedicated rescuers, and G.R.A.C.E. awards (Golden Rescue And Community Excellence) to rescued dogs that had truly found their calling with their new families. This year's winners were:

Andy—certified as an Urban Search and Rescue dog for FEMA
Bentley—a certified therapy dog that has completed one thousand visits to patients
Copper—a drug-sniffing dog; King County's K-9 of the Year in 2006
Tripp—three-legged Tripp saved his family when their house burst into flames; he received the county's first ever Civilian Life Saving award.

Golden Starfish Awards were presented to Nancy and Allan Kiesler of the Evergreen Golden Retriever Club in Washington, and to Jody and Mike Jones of Homeward Bound Golden Retriever Rescue. The name of the award comes from The Starfish Story.

A young man is walking along the ocean and sees a beach on which thousands and thousands of starfish have washed ashore. Further along, he sees an old man, walking slowly and stooping often, picking up one starfish after another and tossing each one gently into the ocean.

"Why are you throwing starfish into the ocean?" he asks.

"Because the sun is up and the tide is going out and if I don't throw them further in, they will die."

"But, old man, don't you realize there are miles and miles of beach and starfish all along it? You can't possibly save them all, you can't even save one-tenth of them. In fact, even if you work all day, your efforts won't make any difference at all."

The old man listened calmly and then bent down to pick up another starfish and throw it into the sea and said:

"It made a difference to that one."

Later in the day, I lined up with other dogs and handlers to have blood drawn for the DNA blood bank. Chatter qualified, since she has a registered pedigree; Daisy with her unknown lineage didn't. For her donation, Chatter received a bright green kerchief that said, "I gave blood for DNA research." Now, both girls sported special recognition of their roles in the day's events.

Margo arrived at the dinner hour with a splendid feast of delectable dishes from a local market, and spread them out for us on the trailer's spacious dining room table. Walter had returned from his photo trip, and we all shared stories from the week. "What a contrast the rainforest was to where we live in the southwest," Walter said. "It's so dense, lush and green. And it rains all the time!"

"We didn't have rain," I said, "but we had cool temps and morning fog. It was perfect weather for the girls, and they did great."

Margo tried to wash her hands in the kitchen sink. "Sorry, Margo. We're out of water, and have been for several days." We laughed about our predicament, thankful that the weather had been cool and we could at least wash our hair with bottled water.

While we discussed our plight, a man dispensing water to RVs from a tanker truck arrived to refill our supply. "Hi there, Mark," Margo greeted him. By now, we realized that Margo knew many people, but this was a real surprise. Mark's wife is a breeder of goldens. Margo told him of our need for water, but he disagreed.

"Heck, there's plenty of water in your tank," he said. "Whoever set up your trailer never leveled it properly, so the pump wouldn't work."

"No way!" Jenny and I exclaimed.

"Yup—I'll top it off for you, but there's plenty here."

We laughed some more, planned to take long showers that night, and turned our attention back to Margo's feast.

But Daisy and I weren't finished yet: The freestyle clinic was scheduled for the evening, as soon as instructor Carolyn Scott arrived from the airport through heavy traffic. We watched videos of sensational performances by award-winning teams in this new sport that is essentially dancing with your dog in a routine choreographed to music. We practiced basic moves and explored the process of matching our dog's personality to music. I concluded right away that Daisy's song would be, "It's Not Where You Start, It's Where You Finish" from the Broadway musical *Seesaw*. Our rally work would be a good foundation for freestyle. We gained another activity to train and practice.

I hugged Jenny and thanked her for being such a good trailer mate and ringside cheerleader. I hugged Margo and applauded our fine meal and the extra grooming she'd done on my girls. I gave thanks for this overwhelmingly satisfying experience, my ever-ready and talented dogs, and to Walter for being so supportive of me and the girls. We got to bring home a new title, several agility Qs and rally successes. How could this trip have been any better?

Trials –
and
Tribulations

Every trial has its own personality. The sponsoring club's members can be friendly, organized, focused, distracted, frenzied, aloof, overburdened or unprepared. Putting on a trial is an enormous amount of work. For months prior to the trial weekend, entries must be processed, the site arranged, judge contracted, workers lined up, and equipment repaired and hauled. During the trial, rings must be set, equipment off loaded, courses set (and changed, over and over again), timing and judging recorded, scores computerized and results posted. Volunteers are the heart and soul of every trial, and must be scheduled and reminded of their duties throughout.

The trial site also plays a big role in the comfort, convenience, beauty and success of the event. Sometimes, everything comes together—preparations, staffing and location—to create a memorable and successful weekend. Other times, it's just a trial to get through the trial. A location in New Mexico has quite a nice covered arena with decent footing and plenty of room for encampments and RV parking. But one

228

March weekend was battered by the frequent spring winds that mark the transition from winter to spring.

The first day was breezy, so we set up our ground mats, cloth crates and chairs just outside the arena on the north side, where we'd be shaded in the afternoon. By Sunday morning, however, the winds began to pick up steam. We re-packed most of our gear and decided to hunker down in our vehicles between runs.

With her usual indifference to weather, Daisy was happy to take long walks around the arena, even though dust and sand from the expansive surrounding parking areas swirled in gusts. Inside the arena, the footing mostly stayed put, while the sand from the parking lot blew straight across the two courses set inside.

But this day, Daisy the Unflappable was distracted, not only by flying debris, but also the numerous pigeons that roosted in the rafters. She was unable to earn a single Q for the weekend. But we were often so close to success that I decided to persevere. Others around me packed it in and headed for home before we were subjected to a full gale. Nope, not us — we were in it for the long haul.

By afternoon, the winds became constant and fierce. The two judges conferred and decided to continue. They voiced their concern that some of the smaller dogs, like papillons, might be blown off the dog walk, so they'd continue to monitor the situation. As the day wore on, one judge advised handlers, "If the jumps blow down while you're on the course, just keep going."

While some dogs lowered their heads to blink the dust out of their eyes, Daisy charged ahead. As if laughing in the face of adversity, her enthusiasm never waned. We stepped up to the start line for every run, hoping for the best. But this wind affected her like it does some horses, especially when it comes from behind and gooses them. She was almost fractious, ripping around the course. I knew I could scarcely be heard, so I had to rely on my hand and body signals. Apparently, they were inadequate, and my girl chased pigeons, sniffed those great horse arena smells, and ripped some more. We stayed to the bitter end, skunked in Qs, but survivors of the experience.

Sometimes, it's the hotel that poses challenges. During our second year at the Scottsdale show, not only did we have to perform well in our events, but we had to maneuver through obstacle courses at the hotel as well.

On arrival, we were given a room on the first floor, as requested, and right by one of the exit doors. Perfect. Easy to take the girls out at night and first thing in the morning. By 11:30 that night, I had a different opinion.

The hotel was packed with other exhibitors, who were doing the same thing, and had to pass by our door to do so. Chatter appointed herself head guard and chief barker, and soon responded to every little sound with a hair trigger. Our room was also next to the elevator that hadn't stopped wheezing between floors since we bedded down. Daisy was annoyed, Chatter was in a tizzy, and Walter wondered what he'd gotten himself into.

I called the front desk to request another room. "Sorry, ma'am," the clerk said. "We're full up tonight, but I'll put you on the list to move first thing in the morning."

In an effort to silence Chatter and let everyone get some sleep, I volunteered to move to the Yukon. At midnight, pillow in hand, I led the very wound-up dog to the car. I retrieved a sleeping bag and a thick dog pad from our cargo trailer and hunkered down. Chatter thought this was dandy and slept well. I didn't.

The next morning, we moved all our gear to room number two. But the refrigerator didn't work. The staff agreed to send a new unit. I answered a knock at the door. There sat a refrigerator, all by itself. I looked up and down the hallway, but didn't see a soul. I called the front desk. "Am I supposed to wrestle this new unit in and the old one out?" "Oh, no, ma'am. I'll send someone right there."

We tried to settle in for the night. When Walter realized that Chatter had her engine running and would likely stay that way, he offered to take her to the Yukon. Tonight would be his turn to camp out in the hotel parking lot. Daisy and I accepted his insistence that we remain in the room. We slept well.

Next day we departed for the trial at 7:00 AM, to find carpet layers already at work, ripping up the entire hallway carpet. "What can they be thinking?" I asked Walter, as we led the girls to the car, trying to avoid the chaos in the hall. "The hotel is full, many guests have dogs with them, and it's high season here in Arizona. Don't you think they could schedule this for August when there's no one in town?"

When we returned after 5:00 that evening, the crew was still hard at work. The fumes from carpet glue filled the hall. We picked our way around workers and carpet rolls to seek solace in our room. After I fed the girls, I stretched out on the bed to rest just a bit before going to dinner. A knock on the door roused the girls for their now well-practiced hotel door alert.

"Excuse me, ma'am," a polite worker inquired, when I opened the door. "Could you please leave your door open, so we can work on the carpet here?"

That was the last straw. I advised him that no, he could not, we'd been gone for the past ten hours, and this was really an inconvenience. I closed the door and fumed, as we dressed for dinner. Then, I was off to the front desk to add this to my growing list of complaints.

To their credit, the hotel did respond to my subsequent letter to management. They reduced our bill by 50 percent, reimbursed me for spoiled food, and included a Starbuck's gift card to boot. It was an appropriate response, but still couldn't erase the bizarre issues that impacted our week. Future stays in Scottsdale will be in another hotel.

Despite the circumstances, the girls did well in competition. They each earned four double Qs toward their RAE titles in rally. They inched toward the required ten double Qs and performed like champs.

The wind kicked up more each morning and provided yet another challenge. One day, while Chatter performed the "honor" position (maintaining a down or sit stay for the duration of another dog's time on the course), a sheaf of judge's papers sailed off the table, scattered across the course, and flew all around her. We eyed each other with deep intensity. "Am I okay?" she seemed to ask. "Yes, you are, and don't move a muscle," my eyes replied. Sure enough, her little bottom remained pinned to the grass, and we earned another Q. I praised her lavishly and hugged her proudly.

At one trial, strong spring winds in New Mexico almost finished me off, in a very ignominious fashion. I'd crossed the wide, grassy soccer field late in the afternoon to use the porta potty. While inside, I began to hear shrieks and howls outside that sounded more like terror than celebration of a great run. Suddenly, the porta potty began to rock violently from side to side. I braced my arms against the panels, and a horrifying image of my possible fate sprang to mind. After a very long fifteen to twenty seconds that felt like half a day, it stopped. I gingerly let go and cautiously opened the door.

A swath of destruction spread from one side of the field to the other, right through the middle. Shade tents were twisted into unrecognizable shapes. Debris was strewn everywhere. Heavy metal ex-pens had been lifted straight up in the air, leaving dogs inside unharmed, but now loose and scared. The microburst demolished the tent right next to mine, but our encampment was untouched. Everyone gathered up dogs, returned far-flung items, tried to straighten out bent and twisted poles, and regain their composure.

Surprisingly, that weekend was one of Daisy's most stellar performances, earning seven Qs out of eight runs. I also felt like I'd grabbed the brass ring, when I dodged Death by Porta Potti.

Back in southwest Colorado, I entered both girls in my club's NADAC agility trial over Labor Day. It would be Chatter's first official trial, and I looked forward to her début. Just a week prior, we'd purchased our first RV and drove it home from Los Angeles. I decided there was no time like the present to initiate it into trial travel.

"Are you sure you're comfortable with it?" Walter asked, while I loaded dog supplies, food and my gear into the closets and storage areas the day before departure.

"Sure. After all, I drove it for four hundred of the eight hundred miles. Why wouldn't I be comfortable?"

"Okay, but you call me if you need any help."

The girls had seen the vehicle parked in our driveway, but had never traveled in it. I opened the side door and said, "Load up!" and in they jumped. I settled in the driver's seat, and the two girls poked their noses into every corner of the RV. They bounded up on the sofa, jumped over to the dinette seats, and scrambled up and down the aisle.

Soon Chatter found her way up next to me and settled between the front seats. Daisy perched atop the sofa, to better view the world through the huge front windows, tongue lolling and grin spreading. "Now you're driving Miss Daisy in style!" she seemed to say.

"Here we go, girls," I announced, released the brake and headed down the driveway. "We're off!"

During the forty-five-minute drive to the trial site in Bayfield, they puttered some more, but generally seemed quite comfortable with their new, very expanded accommodations. We arrived at the site shortly before classes were to begin, so I had little time to set up. I picked a spot in the designated RV section, checked that it was level—whew— I didn't have to fuss with the stacking levelers— and went to walk the course. I left the girls in the RV between their classes, and noticed a distinct difference in Daisy's performance. She seemed more relaxed, more focused and happier than when she was parked ringside in a crate. Another plus to having the RV.

The forecast for the weekend included rain, and by Saturday afternoon, storm clouds thickened over the field. Rain began to drench us all, and didn't let up until Monday morning. The grassy field absorbed it well, and the courses were still safe to run, in between downpours. The RV parking area was a different story.

The hard-packed clay dirt beneath our tires soon turned to gumbo—a thick, slick and deepening moat around each RV. The more experienced RVers had spread artificial turf or outdoor carpet in front of their doors, or let out their awnings, tilted to let rain run off. All I had to work with was a handful of old bath towels—and two very wet, muddy and unperturbed water dogs, ever eager to bound into or out of the moat. I wiped feet, dried fur, spread towels everywhere, hung my rain jacket, and shed my boots—every single time we returned to our abode. Determined not to ruin the interior on our first journey, I couldn't let up for a minute, all weekend long.

During the day, I learned just how much I didn't know about my RV. At first, I couldn't extend the slide out section. A neighboring RV friend helped me troubleshoot. I needed to pull on the parking brake harder, and then it would work.

Saturday night, I was so tired that all I wanted for dinner was whatever I could heat quickly in the microwave. When I couldn't get it to work, I ate the soup cold, right out of the can.

Sunday morning, a hot shower sounded really good. But I couldn't figure out how to turn the water heater on. So, a cold, very abbreviated shower would have to do.

Now, how to dry my hair? Oh, I can't get the wall plugs to work? Okay, towel dry and pull on a baseball cap. Chilly, but at least clean.

Walter planned to bring a small barbeque out on Sunday evening and grill burgers for a group of us. I went from RV to RV, inviting folks to join us. Surprised that we still planned this soggy meal, many declined, preferring to hunker down inside their dry spaces. A couple of folks assumed we wouldn't pursue this foolish plan, and had already eaten. But a hardy few helped us set up the "buffet" from the back of the Yukon, while another volunteered his beach umbrella to shield the grill from the rain. We enjoyed a delicious dinner under the awning of an adjacent RV, as we swapped tales of other challenging trials in ruinous weather.

A month later, in Dolores, a small town about an hour's drive from home, this scene played out again. Durango's average annual rainfall is about nineteen inches. I'm sure most of that year's total fell on Labor Day weekend, plus this one other trial weekend in early October.

I'd already taken the RV on her maiden voyage and survived in the rain, so I confidently loaded the girls inside for the drive to Dolores. The trial site was to die for, courses spread on luxurious grass of superbly maintained baseball fields just outside town. The diamonds that weren't being used were open to us and our dogs, so they could stretch their legs, chase balls, and warm up for their runs. It would be the perfect site.

Except for the rain. Despite a cloudy afternoon on Friday, we were optimistic that we could dodge this storm for the weekend. We set up equipment and prayed for the best.

Since this was a new, small trial, there were only two RVs at the site. The other was a massive, elaborate full-time living vehicle that I'm sure contained a washer and dryer, which I would have appreciated that weekend. A short distance away, sat my little twenty-five-foot Winnebago, a perfect size for me and the two girls—in good weather.

Rain began to spit overnight on Friday, and became a

full-on storm by morning. We emerged yet again into a mud-slicked parking lot, and my eager girls bounded into the mess, brown ooze filling their pads and deepening during the day to engulf their entire paws. "No matter," they seemed to say. "We're water dogs and this is just fine with us!"

The only problem—other than the rain and mud—was that the RV parking was quite a distance from the course. This time, I couldn't just leave them in the RV and fetch them when their runs were due. I borrowed an ex-pen and set them up under the overhang of the vacant snack stand. That plus a small tarp provided them some cover, and they settled down on thick beds that I tucked close to the wall of the building.

Despite the conditions—bad and becoming horrible—it was a very fun trial. Camaraderie born of adversity bloomed, and the small group of handlers cheerfully filled every job. Both girls had truly exceptional runs on the jumper's course, the kind of runs a proud handler remembers for a long, long time. We danced together, like Gene Kelly in *Singin' in the Rain*—gracefully turned corners, and moved smoothly together, as coordinated as we could be. I welcomed their muddy paws all over the front of my jacket when we celebrated afterwards.

Although they both continued to run through the rain with glee, those would be our only two Qs for the weekend. Just the week before, Chatter had overcome her fear of the dog walk, and now it was her favorite obstacle. On every course, she made a beeline for it, pranced across, and back again, to show her new confidence and prowess. Fine with me—at least she's doing it and is happy.

Daisy once again found foul weather just to her liking, perhaps like her ancestral Scotland, where the first goldens were bred. She couldn't contain her enthusiasm, and spun and twirled around the courses. I remembered Lynne's first assessment of her: "My, what nice drive she has." I couldn't fault her wild enthusiasm—we just need to channel it better.

Rally to the Rescue, Maybe

A mind is a terrible thing to waste, and an exercised dog is a happy dog, and every dog needs a job. That's why I pursued rally obedience with both girls, and learned how dramatically different they are. When I look back on our years of training, practice and competition, I can see how far we've come. We really defied the odds.

Daisy's response to any move toward the yard, the garage or the car is always "YES!" My ever-ready girl is nothing if not an enthusiastic participant. She likes to train at warp speed, learn ten new things each day, and seldom shows fatigue or frustration if she's not spot on.

"That means you have to be slower, more precise and very clear with her," Mary reminded me during an early rally class. "Just because she wants to rip through the course doesn't mean you do it that way. Take your time and don't rush."

"Okay." We set up again at the start of the course. Daisy flung her bottom to the ground, threw her head back, tongue flopped out one side, and eyed me with a huge grin.

"Are you ready?" Mary asked, role-playing a judge.

"Yes."

"Forward."

"Daisy, heel." I stepped off toward the first sign on the course, which asked for a sit and stay, while I walked around her. Daisy couldn't believe we'd stopped so soon, and swiveled her head like an owl to watch me.

"Heel." We walked toward a row of four orange cones that required us to serpentine through in tandem. "Come on, that's it." I encouraged her, careful to allow enough space for her to move next to me. "Good girl."

We approached fifteen course cards and executed fifteen different moves. Daisy was exuberant, but remained attentive.

"Hooray for you," Mary said. "See how much better she pays attention when you slow down? You have to be her rock, her anchor. She wants to fly off in all directions, kind of like centrifugal force. When you make her work at a moderate pace, she has time to think, not just react. Now, you're ready for this weekend's trial."

I hoped so. We'd achieved our novice title by earning seventy or more points on three different courses. But that was on leash. This weekend, we'd moved up to the advanced level and Daisy must work off leash. And the course will be set in an arena used for livestock shows, full of enticing smells and the occasional remnant of manure. Heaven help us.

We arrived an hour before our class to walk off nerves, get acclimated to the arena, and socialize with friends and their dogs. Chipper as ever, Daisy was eager to get it on.

The judge for our class was a woman impeccably attired in a blue silk dress, her hair pinned back, and her make-up flawless behind round-rimmed glasses. Holding her clip-board and following each team around the course, she reminded me of a schoolteacher, poised to find any flaws. I tried to mask my trepidation behind a smile when she called our number into the ring.

"Are you ready?"

"Yes, we are." I silently vowed to be Daisy's irresistible main attraction for the next two minutes.

"Forward."

I stepped off and steered Daisy to the first station, then the second and the third. I could feel her engine revving dangerously close to a high whine and then it happened. She careened off course, to explore smells and jump over other stations, and then charged at the judge. Our brief obedience career passed before my eyes in slow motion. I watched in horror as Daisy bounded up to Miss Prim and planted her dirty feet on the judge's shoulders. "Hi! I'm Daisy. Who are you?"

I managed to move my leaden legs and grab Daisy's collar. I was met with an icy stare and words that sounded as if they came from God: "You are excuuused from the ring."

Mortified, I slunk to the exit. I prayed to be swallowed by the earth and transported to the underworld. Daisy continued to bounce, grin and greet friends and strangers outside the ring. My friends smiled, patted Daisy, and put comforting arms across my shoulders. Once again, Daisy's uncontainable enthusiasm had been, well, uncontained.

Despite this embarrassing display, we returned the next day and Daisy was more focused. We had a different judge and we succeeded. We weren't at the top of the class, but we got a passing grade. Whew. We're back on track.

We continued to train, trial and rack up enough solid scores, including some first rate and first place ones, to earn the advanced title and—wonder of wonders—the next level, which is excellent. I was proud of my girl and our partnership and all the hours of class, private sessions and practice that have helped her mature into an impressive competitor.

Next, we embarked on the journey for the big prize: the Rally Advanced Excellent (RAE) title. To achieve this, you must earn a passing score (seventy or higher) on both the advanced and the excellent courses on the same day—and do it ten times. All told, from novice through RAE, we'll have to chalk up twenty-nine qualifying scores. Uncertain if we can do this, I reasoned that at least we'd have fun traveling to trials and spending the weekends with friends. We'd also need divine intervention, many times over.

We gradually piled up the points. Of course, there were some stumbles, too. One spring, when we returned to the scene of her over-the-top judge's greeting, Daisy couldn't complete a course to save her soul. Distracted, unfocused and disconnected from me, she didn't earn a single Q the entire weekend. I pledged to give her some time off and consulted with Mary to rebuild our working relationship. I also acknowledged that many of her errors were really mine. It was back to basics for both of us.

The next year, after we picked up a few more Qs, Daisy returned to the arena with her game face on and confidence galore. We moved together like Fred Astaire and Ginger Rogers. It was magical to see and rewarding to experience. On her last run of the weekend, before an audience of good friends, she achieved perfection: a flawless score of one hundred. We were elated, and her admirers flocked to applaud her excellence.

"Now, we're just one double qualifying round away from our RAE," I told the appreciative circle around us. "I wish it could have been here, but at least you got to see Daisy at her best."

Several weeks later, a large envelope arrived in the mail from the AKC. I wondered what this was. I carefully slit the side and removed a gold embossed certificate that bestowed the RAE title on Gladdogs's Dashing Daisy. I must have lost track of one of those double Qs. We did it! And our friends got to see Daisy earn her title after all.

"Chatter, honey, come on." I coax, pat my leg, and reward her with a treat when she returns to my side. "Now, let's try again. Look." I hold a treat up to my nose, to guide her gaze into mine. "Good girl. Heel." We practice up and down on the parking pad in front of the garage. Then, I throw in an "around" where I turn toward her and she turns toward me, and returns to the heel position on the left side. "Perfect!" Another morsel reinforces her success. "That's all for today. Go play now." Chatter retrieves a ball and we engage in her favorite game.

While Daisy is all big impressions and bravado, Chatter seems forever to ask, "Is that right? Are we okay? Am I okay?" She is the epitome of the clingy, Velcro dog. I think that helping her become proficient in our partnership is just what the doctor would order.

That may be true, but it's going to be a long road to the Promised Land. She takes longer to understand the commands and moves. Training has to be done in very small increments. Her attention span—except for the Holy Grail of the tennis ball—is shorter. Her nerves and insecurity surface quickly. She pants and drools and forgets the simplest commands. She is a tender green shoot that needs patient, gentle nurturing.

We journeyed to Albuquerque for her first official trial. Mary and Gay also entered their dogs, and we appreciated our small support group, set up in one of the noisy halls of the New Mexico State Fairgrounds buildings. From the get go, Chatter was nervous—too many dogs, too much noise, too unsettling an environment. She was on her own, without Daisy's confident demeanor next to her. When we walked outside, she pulled toward the car, away from the building. We all lavished her with attention, tried to comfort her nerves and encourage her success.

I looked at this trip as just a way to get some experience under her belt, and that was the right thing to do. She searched for the exit in every ring and could complete only a few stations each run. "That's okay, honey. You did very well with this challenging place. We won't come back here again."

Our next trials took place in less harried settings, usually outdoors on grass, and she began to blossom. Her new skills bolstered her confidence and we earned some nice scores. While Daisy seemed to lurch between NQs (non-qualifying scores) and the high nineties, Chatter established herself as a solid B student, racked up eighties, and earned novice, advanced, and yes, excellent titles. I could hardly believe we were headed toward the coveted RAE together.

Taking both girls to trials helped me help Chatter. I always tried to run Daisy on the courses first, to see how it felt with a partner alongside. When I stepped up with Chatter, I'd already experienced where the turns were tight, where the distractions were overpowering, and where my girls could each shine. That strategy paid off, as they both gathered points and enjoyed the outings. Even Chatter seemed perky on course, and she loved the attention of friends and new acquaintances.

The weekend Daisy earned her RAE, Chatter earned the eighth leg toward her amazing achievement. With just two more double Qs she would equal her sister's record.

We traveled to Eagle, Colorado for the big event. Jeanne, her breeder, would be there and bring Chatter's mama, Minnie. I looked forward to a joyful family reunion, but also bore the weight of performance anxiety.

The girls and I fired up the motorhome and headed north, over Red Mountain Pass. Fortunately, it was July and the roads were clear. This stretch of highway is the most avalanche-prone road in the United States. During winters, the tiny town of Silverton can be cut off from the rest of the world. Even in summer, the narrow two lanes are treacherous, without roadside barriers or even shoulders along sections. I always hold my breath around tight curves and snakelike switchbacks, praying for no on-coming traffic, so I can hug the centerline. Okay, so I can straddle it. Yes, and even move into the opposite lane.

Daisy loves this road. She stands between the front seats, longing to be a hood ornament, so she can arrive everywhere first. Once she saw a fat marmot waddle across the road right in front of us. For the next forty miles, she stood with her front feet on the passenger's seat, surfed the tight curves, and lusted after the next sighting. This day, we stopped in Grand Junction to run a few errands. Durango's biggest shopping opportunity involves a Super Walmart, so whenever we venture into the neighborhood of a mall, we take advantage. It was over ninety degrees in this lower elevation gateway to the Grand Mesa country, so the air conditioning ran until bedtime at the KOA campground.

The next day, we drove through the dramatic, narrow canyon near Glenwood Springs, gaining elevation along Interstate 70 to Eagle, a small community just forty miles west of mega ski mecca Vail, but still recognizable as a genuine mountain village that takes pride in its small town size and values. They recently sent a proposal for a big box store packing down the road, for now able to preserve their ambiance.

We turned off the highway and dropped down into the river valley to the beautiful, new indoor event center. RVs began to arrive and jockey into position. Inside, the locals set up rings, and early arrivals claimed crate space for their dogs. Over the years, I've learned that Daisy can feel threatened when she's confined in a crate or ex-pen. An animal whisperer once told me that she fears being hurt or stolen, and that's why she feels the need to bark or growl when crated. I've tried everything to resolve this behavior, but have only been able to modify it. I know that Daisy is a bit like Greta Garbo—"I vant to be alone"—so I snagged a spot by the wall where she wouldn't be startled or annoyed when other dogs and handlers passed behind her. I brought the girls inside to get the lay of the land.

"Daisy, this is just a walk in the park for you. You've already got your Ph.D. in rally. But Chatter, Little Miss, this is your stage for The Big Show. I know you can do it." *Sure, don't put any pressure on her or myself.*

We took afternoon and evening strolls on the grounds

and in the meadow by the river. The girls snuggled on the bed next to me and we dreamed of success.

The next day, Jeanne and Linda arrived and we sat ringside for the conformation judging of the goldens. A wealth of information and experience, Jeanne noted the fine points and flaws of so many beautiful dogs that it made my head spin. They all looked stunning to me.

At eight years old, Minnie's face was totally white and the rest of her thick coat would catch up soon. Sweet, calm and polite, Minnie settled quietly at Jeanne's feet, an old hand at the routine of shows. She won a top prize at last year's golden national specialty and has many other field and obedience titles.

I left Daisy to doze in the RV. Chatter seemed pleased to be my only dog for the moment, and I hoped she could channel some of her mom's confidence and contentment. She exhibited decent manners, in spite of the sensory stimulation of multiple rings, judges, and lots and lots of dogs and people.

Afternoon arrived and obedience classes began. Daisy performed with her usual verve. She sped around the ring and earned nice scores that could be the start of a second RAE, should I decide to pursue it. Chatter followed me tentatively around the course. I had to slow down, urge her to keep up, and plead for her attention. Even so, she qualified on both runs. One day down, one to go.

Over dinner that night, Jeanne and Linda coached me. "Your girls are so different," Jeanne pointed out. "You need to slow down with Daisy. Don't let her set the pace. But with Chatter, you need to speed up. You know she's Velcro, so she won't want to be left behind. She'll pull herself together to keep up with you and will perform better."

I drifted off to sleep repeating these wise words from a pro in the business. *Let it be so tomorrow.*

Morning dawned clear, but winds were forecast for later. We took long walks, visited with friends, and I prepared for the afternoon. At lunch in the RV, I noticed the wind had picked up and I battened down all the hatches. The girls snoozed, unperturbed.

Unpredictable Rocky Mountain weather blew in, and competitors departed as soon as their classes ended. Jeanne and Linda apologized for getting a jump on their drive home, but wished us well. The few folks I'd recognized from other shows also pulled out. We were on our own now, alone together, our years of practice on the line.

As events finished in each ring, stewards folded up the white lattice perimeters, stacked up chairs, and took down tables. Once crowded, the arena looked empty now. It felt like rats were deserting a sinking ship. Winds howled outside. Vendors packed up their wares and pulled down their canopies. Larger gusts assaulted the arena, and the few folks still there wrestled with open doors to shut them against the force.

Both girls seemed oddly content in their exercise pen. I patted and treated them. We awaited our turn in the cavernous space. One by one, they both racked up high marks on the excellent course. Only the advanced class remained and Chatter would complete the long road to her RAE.

A huge gust roared furiously outside, followed by the sound of wrenching metal and snapping canvas. A massive vendor tent whipped into an unrecognizable tangle. I peered out a crack in a door to be sure my RV was still standing. This began to feel dangerous.

Miss Unflappable, Daisy marched around the advanced

course with a flourish and earned a tidy ninety points. I hugged her and rewarded her effort with a handful of treats. I shuttled her into the pen, slipped off her leash, and put it on Chatter. "Okay, darlin', this is it. Not the conditions I would have chosen, but this is what we have, so this is what we'll do."

We walked around the arena, now deserted except for our ring in one corner and the photographer's set-up at the other end.

"You're not leaving yet are you?" I inquired of the two photographers, as they tried to rearrange blown down potted plants and signboards on their platform.

"No way. Not until every class has ended."

"Good. Because I hope to have a new title holder for you soon."

We returned to the ring and I stepped off from the start line, Jeanne's advice fresh in my mind. Chatter moved right alongside me, heeled closely, sat on command, and completed turns, circles and serpentines like a champ. Wind howled, dust billowed near the doorways, and unseen things bumped and banged against the arena walls. Chatter never wavered, never hesitated, never left my side. All too soon, we stepped past the finish line, and I could breathe again.

"That was wonderful!" Chatter jumped up to get a big hug. "That was amazing! What a fabulous run! Let's see what your score is."

I paced by the ringside easel, anxious for the steward to post our score. Soon, she penned a ninety-five next to Chatter's entry number.

"Chatter, you were brilliant! Thank you for doing your absolute best under very difficult conditions." I grabbed

Daisy from the pen and we all jogged toward the photographers' corner.

"We did it! Here's a new RAE title holder and her sister, who got hers this spring."

"That's wonderful," Jan said. "We've done a lot of obedience ourselves, so we understand what goes into success like that. They're not just pretty faces." She winked at me.

We managed to get the excited dogs to sit on the platform in front of me, with the kind and patient judge alongside them. But every time the photographer tossed her fur-covered toy in the air, to get the dogs' attention, Chatter launched off to get it.

"Well, she is a retriever," the judge said. "Let her keep it in her mouth and see if that works."

"We can't have that," the photographer said. "It looks like she's caught a rat. We'll just pretend to throw it and I'll be very fast." The judge and I posed, Daisy stayed in place and, for one very split second, so did Chatter.

"Got it." The photographer grinned. "Those sure are beautiful dogs. Congratulations to all of you."

"Many thanks. I'll cherish this photo, for sure."

I started doing rally to build our working relationships and have another fun thing to do together. It had been a years-long process, with lots of ups and downs along the way. I had to learn to read and train each girl to match her needs and abilities.

I never expected to gain so much. Success built upon success, and I could see confidence and pride emerge. Training became so enjoyable for all of us that it was more a game than work.

Now that I've mounted those photos and hard-won certificates on the wall, we'll turn our attention back to agility and add freestyle to our repertoire. Friends and admirers often commented after our rally runs that it looked like we were dancing out there. Since freestyle is choreographed heeling set to music, thanks for the suggestion. And yes, we'd love to dance. Maybe just not with a tornado outside.

Chatter Whispers

"She's been abused," the woman said, as she stood next to Chatter, her hand resting lightly on the dog's head. "She was hit with newspapers. And a man tried to strike her with a bat or maybe a length of pipe. But he missed and hit the wall or something else."

Her words engulfed and saddened me. I couldn't imagine my sweet, tender girl ever being subjected to any wrath, let alone what she described. This knowledge would begin to explain things I hadn't been able to understand.

We were in Tucson at an agility trial. Daisy was having a splendid weekend, after a splashy entrance Friday night. On her first run, she raced at warp speed through the tunnels, and even managed to slow and collect herself before the weave poles and complete those with verve. But, once again, her need for speed intervened and she threw in some remarkable spins and twirls that weren't in the course design. I could only laugh, as I gathered her in my arms and praised her pizzazz. Joy gleamed in her eyes, and I knew she was ready for anything.

By contrast, Chatter struggled Friday and again all

day Saturday. Despite her capabilities practiced at home, she couldn't remain focused, and wandered aimlessly on the courses before seeking the exit from the ring. I was so puzzled that I sought the advice of The Animal Whisperer. Set among a row of vendors at the trial, the lean and lithe woman with long gray hair and a soft demeanor might help me unlock the secret to Chatter's struggles.

"I'd like you to ask her two questions," I began. "How does she feel about agility, and what does she want to do with the rest of her life?"

The woman paused, touched Chatter with a gentle hand, and waited for an answer to arise from the little blonde.

She revealed the abuse almost immediately. Then, I learned that Chatter likes agility, but because of her abusive history, sometimes she loses herself on the course. "It's almost as if she hears a giant roar in her head, and she literally can't hear you over that," the woman advised. *Sort of like post traumatic stress disorder. Something triggers the fear and she can't overcome it.*

"But she loves you more than anything and would do whatever you ask, if only she could." I nodded, a lump in my throat.

"And she'd like to be a medical intuitive," the woman announced. "She wants to be able to help people."

"I've been thinking about getting back into animal-assisted therapy," I said. "Maybe this is the perfect time."

"Yes, she'd like that."

All through our half hour discussion, Chatter lay quietly at our feet, undisturbed by the constant flow of people and dogs passing by. She seemed peaceful and content.

That night, I began to put some pieces together. Maybe that's why Chatter had been so afraid to get in the back of the car; she knew that the harsh sound of the door closing would follow. That fear lingered with her for years and sometimes still crosses her face.

And the teeter. She's always been afraid to complete the teeter. She begins to go on the up side with enthusiasm, but freezes at the fulcrum. Even with many months of gentle training, and my slowly lowering the down side for her, she remains overcome by it. Of course! It bangs when it hits the ground.

Sunday I approached the courses with her a little differently, with my newly acquired insights. I stayed close by, so she could see me clearly. I figured if she began to hear the roar in her head, maybe my presence could help ground her. I promised her that whatever she did on the course was fine with me. And I whispered in her ear at the start line, "I'm right here for you, honey. Let's go have fun and do it together."

Chatter was splendid, absolutely splendid. We had the best day at a trial that we've ever had, earned three Qs, and she seemed to shine.

I reported the results to the whisperer at the end of the day. She smiled. "I'm not surprised. Chatter felt that she was heard yesterday. She unburdened herself of issues that she's carried all her life. Then she was able to move through the world in a different way today."

Back home, I contacted friend and trainer Julie with this story. "I wouldn't be surprised," she said. "If any of those traumatic events happened to her during weeks eight through twelve or thirteen of her life, they occurred during the 'fear period.' Often those will stay with the dog for the rest of her life, no matter how carefully we try to correct them."

I got in touch with Jeanne, her breeder. I brushed aside my concern that she might think me odd for getting such a consult. But I was surprised. Jeanne reported that on occasion she had also sought feedback from whisperers about dogs, and sometimes they provided useful information. She thought that might be the case here. When Chatter had been returned, Jeanne observed some behaviors that might have suggested abuse.

I have no way to corroborate this information further. I know little of the whisperer's credentials. I'd never seen her before or since. But she may have unlocked some of Chatter's past that will help me help her. I've pledged to Chatter that there will be no more teeters in her future, ever. But I still have to close the back of the Yukon, just a little more gently now.

Where Are They Now?

Animal behaviorist and trainer Suzanne told me, when she assessed some of Chatter's wild behaviors at age three, that larger dogs don't really get their full brain power until they're four. I agree with most of her observations gleaned from many years with dogs, but my question for Suzanne now is: What's up with Daisy and Chatter?

At seven and a half, Daisy is the well-behaved companion in the household. Whoever thought I'd be able to say that? She's confident and competent in agility and, except for the occasional quirk, skilled at rally. But her erratic recalls at home mean she can seldom hike off leash with us, like all our other goldens have been able to do. She still hears the call of the wild over and above anything I might ask of her, and charges off to investigate. But she's talented and loving, and has the most beautiful agate-speckled brown eyes. Just beware of her breath if she's been noshing in the yard.

Daisy has also added small birds to her dining repertoire. This spring, many pine siskins and goldfinches gathered around our bird feeders. She watches intently from inside, and charges out the doors, hoping to catch a slow flyer lifting off the deck.

One morning she did. We'd observed a mildly disabled bird at the feeders for a few days. Arriving late, and staying later, the creature seemed to be feeding well, but had some problems taking off and landing. But she hung in there and we admired her gumption.

I developed the habit of looking for her before I let my bird dogs out, but on this morning, I missed her huddled form next to the house. Daisy, however, had not, and scooped up the helpless bird in one fast swoop. I watched, horrified, as Daisy chomped about three times and swallowed. That was it. Wild kingdom, right in my backyard. I was determined not to let that happen again to a bird I'd lured to a feeder.

Now practiced and skilled, Daisy was obsessed. Despite my careful habits, she grabbed another one, right under my watchful eye. "Oh, no you don't!" I fumed. She paused and looked at me, one tiny wing protruding from her lips. "Drop it!" I demanded. She stared me down, but at least didn't chomp.

I approached and grabbed her snout, pried her jaws open and pointed her nose toward the deck. I shook her head and out plopped a soggy little pine siskin, landing on the deck with a tiny thud. Daisy, to her credit, didn't resist me, and stood to watch the small bird regain its composure. Comparisons with Jonah and the Whale seemed appropriate. What a story this bird had to share with its kin.

Fearless as Daisy is when she approaches, investigates, chases and, yes, sometimes devours wildlife, she met her match recently. Although she's a friendly, congenial walking partner, who likes to meet and greet people and dogs, anyone or anything that passes the front of her property is asked to leave post haste. Of course, her speed and vocal insistence always do the trick, since every perambulator does indeed approach, pass by and depart. Daisy assumes she's batting a thousand and is very pleased with her track record.

But the roller skier had her flummoxed. During the last days of autumn, before any real snow had accumulated at the Nordic areas, a fit and friendly gentleman began to park just a few driveways south of our place and prepare for the season by roller skiing up and down the twelve-mile valley. Faster than a man afoot, and displaying fine Nordic form with free-swinging arms and poles, he sped past our place and later returned.

Stunned, Daisy hardly knew what voice to use: Full-throated-car-chasing barks? There's-a-dog-going-by insistence? Person-plus-dog-deserves-extra-effort from the vocal chords? She mustered a What-the-heck-is-this?? bark, strangled by a throat-tightening warble the likes of which I'd never heard from her. I can only assume she thought it was a prehistoric pterodactyl and she used her best other worldly yodel. It worked, too. After just a couple of days, the "beast" never re-appeared. I told Daisy that snow fell, he went to the mountains, and he likely will be back next fall.

At six, Chatter has so far disproved Suzanne's theory. Able to gather herself together most times on rally courses, she earned her big title. Competing in agility, she's still tentative. Her fragile confidence can undermine her composure in a heartbeat. I remind myself that it's her heart and soul I treasure most, and have learned to live with everything else—except when she springs up to grab my hair in her teeth and pull. That's still unacceptable.

Progress with Chatter is unpredictable. There are days when we practice agility that she amazes me with her attention and ability. Totally capable and proficient on most of the obstacles, she can complete a course with ease. But last week, while we practiced twelve weave poles, instead of the novice level six, she became so full of angst at having to repeat them that she careened off the course and into the newly filled, seductive pond. She ignored my calls and swam and swam. I didn't want to witness and therefore reward the behavior, so I hid behind a shed to watch. Unperturbed at being alone, Chatter continued her inaugural swim of the season for several more minutes. The inside of my Subaru looked like it'd been hosed down after she finally returned and shook on the way home.

But the depth of her love and the sweetness of her spirit captivate us. In that regard, she certainly channels Sophie. Yes, the racing stripe on her nose stands for speed, and she can nearly match Daisy's flat out dashes. But she's the equal of any of our dogs in giving and receiving that golden hallmark of true and deep affection.

The others are usually at Big Rock. A massive, angular, lichen-covered boulder the size of a small sedan rests about half way up our property, above the barn and paddock and below the rock-faced cliffs. For some reason, I've always felt this was the physical and spiritual center of our land. From the very beginning, I liked to hike up the hill to sit on Big Rock and survey the valley and river below. The high country looms to the right, with snow-crested peaks all winter, burnished golden flanks in autumn, and deep greens in summer. Usually, a dog or two joins me to sit on the rock and survey our domain.

It's where I go to burst with joy at just getting to be here. It's also where I've gone to connect with special spirits when my heart aches. It's where I sat the afternoon that Jenny and Dave said the final farewell to their beloved Poppi. When I gazed northwestward, toward them in Washington, a small break in a very dark, overcast sky let a brief ray of sun through. *Ahh,* I sighed. *That was Poppi on her way to heaven.*

It's where all my golden spirits spend time. Sometimes it's where they linger, to watch over us. Sophie and Tucker reside there pretty permanently. Bodie breezes in from one of his far-flung wildernesses and pauses before his next dash.

Nikki used to be there, but has now moved on. Yes, she still drops in, and is always instantly with me when I ask her advice or invite her comforting presence. Otherwise, she resides right at the side of God, having completed her many incarnations on earth and achieving a state few will ever know.

Back on earth, blessed to live more days and years in this special place, I continue to wonder why Daisy and Chatter, these two opposites, these two needy and demanding dogs are in my life at the same time, competing for my attention, my love and every bit of training skill I have. They must be here to nudge me out of bed early, to lure me outside to exercise with them, to keep me on my toes, and to share their joy. For that I give thanks, and know that they're every bit as golden as Nikki, Bodie, Sophie and Tucker, and any future retrievers that may join us at the Glad Dog Ranch. Pure gold, indeed. And blessings all.

Looking
in the
Rear View Mirror

As I drove into town recently, on a crisp November afternoon, I glanced in the rear view mirror. Directly behind me was an aged Chevy truck, probably once some shade of yellow or tan, but now just the color of faded grass. The driver, a man, wore a plaid shirt, baseball cap and a neatly trimmed gray beard.

Beside him on the front seat, undoubtedly an old-fashioned bench style, were two golden retrievers. The one in the middle of the seat appeared to be comfortably slumped against him, content to take in the day, as it rolled into view.

But on the passenger side, a gray-muzzled girl, I'm assuming, not only sat upright, but also leaned into the windshield, gathering in the sights with gusto. Her grin spread from ear to ear, her nose tilted slightly upward, and her expression pure joy. She couldn't have expressed herself more clearly if she'd thrown her head back to let loose a throaty laugh.

This glimpse of the two goldens and their person has stayed with me for days. I believe it's the perfect image of life with these remarkable dogs.

Now, when I look in my own rear view mirror, at my years with goldens, that's what I see. We're all throwing our heads back, laughing with joy, and savoring every minute of the ride.

—Holli Pfau
Durango, CO

Acknowledgments

My heartfelt gratitude goes to:

+ Everyone who has taken the journey with me;

+ Jenny Hamilton, Margo Smith and Nancy Sommers for first reads of the manuscript and thoughtful comments;

+ Friends Gay Robson, Sandee Kennedy and DeVere Keen Gamble for encouragement;

+ Teacher, friend and mentor, Will Gray;

+ My agent, Toni Lopopolo, for believing in the dogs;

+ Gail M. Kearns for superb editing and shepherding;

+ My dear husband, Walter, for unwavering support;

+ Nikki, Bodie, Sophie, Tucker, Daisy and Chatter for all the love.

This book honors all of you and celebrates the joyful bond we share with our dogs.

In Memoriam: Larry Cohen, DVM
The best doc in town is with so many friends
at the Rainbow Bridge.

Inspired by the efforts of Golden Retriever Rescue, Holli wrote *Pure Gold* to increase awareness of the joys, challenges and rewards of living with rescued dogs.

A share of the proceeds from *Pure Gold* will support golden retriever and other rescue and adoption efforts. A special program, Fundraising for Rescue, is available to those organizations. Go to www.puregoldbook.com for details.